Debating the Zeitgeist and Being Second Generation

Edited by

MIRIAM E. DAVID and **MERILYN MOOS**

VALLENTINE MITCHELL
LONDON • CHICAGO

First published in 2021 by Vallentine Mitchell

Catalyst House,
720 Centennial Court,
Centennial Park, Elstree WD6 3SY, UK

814 N. Franklin Street,
Chicago, Illinois,
60610 USA

www.vmbooks.com

This edition © Vallentine Mitchell 2021
Individual chapters © contributors 2021
Three poems from Sophie Herxheimer's collection
Velkom to Inklandt (Short Books, 2017) reproduced by
kind permission of the author.

British Library Cataloguing in Publication Data:
An entry can be found on request

ISBN 978 1 912676 84 2 (Paper)
ISBN 978 1 912676 85 9 (Ebook)

Library of Congress Cataloging in Publication Data:
An entry can be found on request

CONTENTS

Notes on Contributors

Miriam E. David Born in 1945, in West Yorkshire, and studied sociology at Leeds University (with Maggie Gravelle – see below), graduating in 1966. Now Professor Emerita of Sociology of Education at University College London (UCL) Institute of Education, she has researched and taught sociology and education at various universities in the UK (and North America). She has published widely in the field, including *Closing the Gender Gap: Postwar Educational and Social Change* with Madeleine Arnot and Gaby Weiner (see below) (Cambridge: Polity Press, 1999) and *A Feminist Manifesto for Education* (Cambridge: Polity Press, 2016). She has also written an intellectual biography *Personal and Political: feminisms, sociology and family lives* (London: Institute of Education Books, 2003), and a memoir *Reclaiming Feminism: challenging everyday misogyny* (Bristol: Policy Press, 2016). Her more recent work is on higher education, and includes *Feminism, Gender and Universities: politics, passion and pedagogies* (London: Taylor & Francis, 2014) and *The SAGE Encyclopedia of Higher Education* (4 vols), co-edited with Dr Marilyn Amey of Michigan State University, USA (Thousand Oaks, California & London: SAGE, 2020). She has also written some short pieces and reviews for the *Association of Jewish Refugees* (AJR) magazine including Journey around my father: Retracing my Jewish roots in Germany, *AJR* 2009 vol 9 no 2 February, p.4 and in 2009 My German Jewish genealogy for *Second Generation Voices* 41 May p 4-5.

Merilyn Moos Born 1944 in Oxford, grew up in Durham where attended Grammar School, then BA in PPE at St. Anne's, Oxford and MA in Contemporary Cultural Studies under Stuart Hall at CCCS (where MA thesis published). 1966-2009 Taught Sociology in Further Education, then HE. Many articles on post-16 education published. Publications include: *The Language of Silence* (London: Writersworld, 2011), a semi-autobiographical novel: *Beaten but not*

Defeated (London: Chronos, 2014) a biography of Siegfried Moos, a German active anti-Nazi and my father and *Breaking the Silence. Voices of the British Children of Refugees from Nazism* (New York & London: Rowman and Littlefield 2015); *Anti-Nazi Germans* (with Steve Cushion) *Enemies of the Nazi State from within the Working Class Movement,* (London: Community Languages and the Socialist History Society, 2020) plus many articles and talks to conferences and gatherings, including a Second Generation Conference, Cologne, a conference about the children of refugees, Berlin, a conference 'Exile and Gender', London, and a conference on 'The Cultural Politics of Memory', Cardiff. Various articles and reviews published in the Second Generation (2GN) 'Voices' and in the AJR bulletin.

Alice Bondi has been a temp typist, teacher, shepherd, environmental interpretation officer, homeopath, lecturer and psychotherapist. For the last 38 years, she has lived 'far from the madding crowd' (the nearest house is a mile away), where she has created what is becoming a woodland; survived winters with snow drifts blocking her route out; delighted in a huge range of wildlife; and welcomed friends from far and wide for whom she loves to cook. Now retired, she finds herself busier than ever (other than during past lambing times) with contributions to various feminist and lesbian campaigns, local community projects, singing in a chamber choir (sadly only via online projects during Covid-19), doggedly vegetable gardening at 1,200 feet, and entertaining her (currently three) cats, who are, of course, the prime movers in everything.

Peter Crome's mother and father came to the UK in 1939 and 1926 respectively and he was born in Italy and grew up in South London. After medical school he trained as a geriatrician at Guy's Hospital before becoming a Consultant in Orpington. He then became a Senior Lecturer at Kings College London and moved to Keele University as Professor of Geriatric Medicine in

1994. He held a variety of Board Positions in the NHS and University and served as Head of the Medical School. He was elected as President of the British Geriatrics Society and the Section of Geriatrics and Gerontology at the Royal Society of Medicine. His clinical and research activities encompassed medical conditions in later life including stroke and dementia. He moved to London in 2012 and holds an Honorary Chair at UCL. He is married to Ilana, an Academic Addiction Psychiatrist, with whom he assisted in writing papers and co-editing a book. He has a son who lives in Israel (Media Strategist) and two children (a lawyer and a public health practitioner) from an earlier marriage. He has been a member of the Labour Party for 40 plus years and first joined a Trades Union over 55 years ago. He was Treasurer of the International Brigade Memorial Trust and now is a Patron. He has written an autobiographical piece https://www.bgs.org.uk/bgs-presidents-biographical-sketches-peter-crome

Irena Fick was born in London of German refugee parents. The family moved back to Germany when she was three, where she grew up. She moved back to Britain when she was 22 and studied at York University as a mature student. After graduating, she qualified as an early childhood teacher and did an M.A. in Comparative Education, comparing changes in Soviet and Chinese language policy. She was an active trade unionist and involved in various disputes at work which didn't do her 'career' any good. After working as a full-time National Official for the Film and Television Union she did her Diploma in Translation and set herself up as a freelance translator and interpreter. Being a backroom-person her political activity has consistently been working on newsletters, starting with the Women's Liberation Workshop newsletter *Shrew*, via the National Assembly of Women, Britain-GDR Society, and *Second Generation Network* newsletters. She now works on the newsletter of the *Older Feminist Network* and does research for the London Socialist Film Society. She contributes articles and chapters to German and English publications on women in the anti-fascist resistance; at present her main interest is in women in the French and Italian resistance, she intends to find out more about women in the Greek and Yugoslav resistance.

Sybil Gilbert was born 1948 in Birmingham where her parents met and put down roots. She was educated at King Edward V1 High School, where she was encouraged to be an independent thinker, read law at King's College, London and, later, obtained a master's research degree from Warwick University. She qualified as a barrister but spent the majority of her working life as a university lecturer. Her main areas of interest were the criminal process, evidence gathering by law enforcement agencies and the reconciliation of these activities with due process and human rights. She has spoken at conferences and published in academic and professional law journals. She has authored several books and contributed chapters to others. Her authored books are (in the name of Sybil Sharpe) *Electronically Recorded Evidence* (London: Fourmat Publishing, 1991), *Judicial Discretion and Criminal Investigation* (London: Sweet and Maxwell, 1998), *Search and Surveillance; The movement from evidence to information* (London: Routledge, 2000 and reissued 2017) and *National Security, Personal Privacy And The Law* (London: Routledge, 2020). She continues to take an active interest in the field of human rights and, in the light of current political developments, how far such rights can protect against populist trends towards 'othering' and discrimination. She has lodged family papers with the Wiener Institute Library in the hope that her family's story will, in its own small way, assist in refuting Holocaust denial (https://wiener.soutron.net/Portal/Default/en-GB/RecordView/Index/70297# The Gross family documents are number 1183).

Maggie R. Gravelle was born in 1945 in Sheffield and studied Sociology at Leeds University, (with Miriam David), graduating in 1966. Now retired, she spent much of her working life as a teacher in both primary and secondary schools, specialising in working with children for whom English was not their first language. She was active in promoting anti-racist, multicultural education and published widely in the field, including two books, *Supporting Bilingual Learners in Schools* (Stoke-on-Trent: Trentham, 1996) and *Planning for bilingual learners: an inclusive curriculum* (ed), (Stoke-on-Trent: Trentham, 2000). In 1994 she became a senior lecturer and subsequently programme leader in the School of Education, University of Greenwich. She has been an Advisor to the QCA and represented the University on several international projects concerned with literacy development. Two short biographical papers about her parents (Kurt Hoselitz and Annemarie Hoselitz (née Meyer)) were chiefly for the family but have also been lodged with the Wiener Library.

Sophie Herxheimer is an artist and poet and has held residencies for LIFT, Museum of Liverpool, The Migration Museum and Transport for London. Exhibitions include The Whitworth, Tate Modern, The Poetry Library and The National Portrait Gallery. She's illustrated five fairy tale collections, made several artists books, created a 300 metre tablecloth to run the length of Southwark Bridge, featuring hand printed food stories from a thousand Londoners; narrated an episode of The Food Programme from Margate, made a life size concrete poem in the shape of Mrs Beeton sited next to her grave; and a pie big enough for seven drama students to jump out of singing, on the lawn of an old people's home. An ongoing project is collecting stories live in ink from members of the public, by listening and drawing. Recent publications include *Your Candle Accompanies the Sun* (Henningham Family Press, 2017) *Velkom to Inklandt* (Short Books, 2017) and (with Chris McCabe) *The Practical Visionary* published by Hercules Editions.

Sophie teaches for The Royal Drawing School and has contributed a chapter to their new book with Thames and Hudson *Ways of Drawing*. Her latest collection, *60 Lovers to Make and Do*, is published with Henningham Family Press.

Janet Leifer born in 1945, grew up in Morden, South London, studied European Studies, majoring in French and, later in life, a MA in Library and Information Studies. Her career was spent working in libraries at Chatham House, Barnet FE College and Immanuel College, a Jewish school in Bushey. Now retired but volunteers at the Jewish Museum in Camden and the Alpine Club Library and tutors children for Barnet Refugees Service. On marriage, migrated from South to North London, and Finchley: widowed with two grown up sons and one stepson, all married, and grandchildren.

Ines Newman studied Politics, Philosophy and Economics at Oxford and then Town Planning at UCL. She started work as a planner with Westminster City Council, but children cut short a traditional career and she subsequently became one of the first job sharers in the UK in 1975, working for the Joint Docklands Action Group (JDAG) as an advocate planner, researcher and community development officer. She moved into economic development, first at the London Borough of Hackney and from 1988 as Head of the Economic Development Unit at Harlow District Council. From 1992 she combined this job with the co-ordinator of the South East Economic Development Strategy Group (SEEDS). In 1998 she was appointed as Head of Policy at the Local Government Information Unit (LGiU). In 2007 she took up a part time post in the Local Government Centre at the University of Warwick and currently has an Honorary Senior Research position at De Montfort University. Throughout her life she has combined academic research and writing with activism. She has written many articles and two books: *Reclaiming Local Democracy* (Bristol: Policy Press, 2014); *Internment in 1940: Life and Art Behind the Wire* (London: Vallentine Mitchell, 2020).

Eric Sanders is a centenarian. Born to Jewish parents in 1919 as Ignaz Erich Schwarz, the gifted pianist and composer was forced to leave Austria after the Anschluss in 1938. In *Secret Operations: From Music to Morse and beyond* (London: History Web, 2010) he presents an inspiring story about his years before the Second World War in Vienna, his flight to the UK and his life after the war, including his work for the Association of Jewish Refugees (AJR), teaching, writing and involvement in Labour party politics.

Clare Ungerson, Emeritus Professor, was born and brought up in London. Her mother came to the UK from Stuttgart in 1936 and her father, also Jewish, was born in Soho, London. She went to primary and secondary schools in London, and, after GCE O Levels, a different secondary school in Birkenhead on Merseyside. She read Philosophy, Politics and Economics as an undergraduate at the University of Oxford and was a postgraduate student of Social Policy at the London School of Economics. She then worked in various London based research institutes, including the Institute of Race Relations and the Centre for Environmental Studies. In the early 1970s she was appointed to a Lectureship in Social Policy at the University of Kent in Canterbury. There she developed an interest in Women's Studies and in a gendered analysis of Social Policy. In 1994 she was appointed Professor of Social Policy at the University of Southampton. She retired in 2005, at age 60, in order to care for her mother, then in her early 90s and living alone in London. In 2006 Clare began a retirement project investigating the previously untold story of a refugee camp for nearly 4000 German speaking Jewish men who were rescued by the Central British Fund for German Jewry to an old first world war camp in Sandwich in East Kent. This was published, by the History Press, as *Four Thousand Lives: the rescue of German Jewish men to Britain, 1939*, in 2014 and reprinted in paperback in 2019. Clare lives in Sandwich where, amongst other things, she is Secretary of the Sandwich and District Labour Party.

Gaby Weiner has held a number of professorial and honorary academic and teaching positions in the UK and retains a professorial link with Umeå University in Sweden where she was professor of teacher education between 1998 and 2005. She has written and edited a number of publications on social justice, gender, race and ethnicity including: *Just a Bunch of Girls* (1985), *Feminisms in Education* (1994); *Closing the Gender Gap: Postwar Educational and Social Change* (Cambridge: Polity Press 1999, with M. Arnot & M. David), and *Kids in Cyberspace*: (2005, with C. Gaine). Her most recent publications include an investigation of the uses of auto/biography in educational research, *Reconstructing and Deconstructing Lives* (2010, with L. Townsend), an overview for the European Commission of research on gender and education in Europe (2010) and a book on the refugee experiences of her family, *Tales of Loving and Leaving* (2016).

Charlotte Williams (née Prager) grew up in South London. She got a B.Sc in Sociology in what is now Buckinghamshire University and has worked in psychiatric care, theatre administration, group work and print management, as well as editor, typesetter and publications manager. She has always been fascinated by learning how other people tick and this has taken her into the world of psychotherapy, where she now works in private practice and also with homeless people in a shelter in London. She lives in Lewes.

Foreword by Lord Dubs

I am not a second-generation immigrant to the UK. I came here from what was then Czechoslovakia in 1939, one of the hundreds of children whose lives were rescued from the clutches of the Nazis by the kindertransport. But I do come from mixed heritage – my father was a Jew from Bohemia and my mother was Austrian. Growing up in Czechoslovakia my mixed heritage wasn't unusual – the enormous Austro-Hungarian Empire had left people scattered and borders had shifted and changed – it was a melting pot.

Of course, my family reflects the wider story of Europe – a continent that has witnessed mass migrations and large-scale immigration, over centuries. This is especially true for Europe's Jewish communities who through persecution and prejudice have been regularly uprooted and forced to find new places of safety and start over again. Today's Europe is little different. Over a quarter of the British people born in the UK today have at least one foreign-born parent, just as my children do and just as I did. Which means this book, although broadly focused on the second generation of migrants created by the Second World War, remains highly topical today. Europe is now facing the greatest refugee crisis since the Second World War. With no prospect of global conflicts or persecution ceasing any time soon, the crisis is set to continue. And with the growing threat to the world's poorest communities of climate change, the refugee crisis and global migration will only increase, as drought, crop failure and flooding drive even more people from their homes.

My story, and the story of those second-generation migrants in this book, will soon be replaced with new stories, new families and different new beginnings. What links many of these stories, as the very personal accounts in this book attest, is trauma. I am reminded of my last visit to the Moria refugee camp on Lesbos, which earlier this year was destroyed by fire.

Many of the children I met there carried their trauma in the often self-inflicted scars on their faces. But trauma isn't always visible. It can be expressed in the things that are not said; the silences born of tragedy that reach into families and down generations. And it can be manifested in the 'otherness', the rootlessness and insecurity that migrant families can continue to feel even decades after making a new home and starting again. Many continue to feel like outsiders – especially when a hostile environment directs its hostility towards them.

This book is not a study about the second generation but gives voice to the second generation themselves. It provides fascinating and unique insights as to how the 'second generation' feels about themselves and their place within their communities. How did it feel to be the only Jewish child at school? How did it feel to have parents, whether or not Jewish, who often wished their children to be more English than the English? How, as happened to my own mother, does it feel to face discrimination because of your foreign background? What do the children of migrants to this country now feel about their parents and the journeys they took? Many of the contributors, though they have built successful and happy lives, still comment that they feel like 'outsiders'. It is as if they are standing in the doorway of a house but do not feel they are welcome within. And others still feel acutely the loss of a background – grandparents, family friends, symbols people and places that anchor them to where they live. They feel uprooted even within their own lives. It's not a book about victimhood, however, quite the opposite. The contributors include those inspired by the anti-Nazi activities of their German parents as well as those who see themselves as people who have come to terms with and learnt from their families' pasts. I am struck by how many of the contributors have dedicated their lives to educating others, campaigning on behalf of the 'outsider' and actively creating a fairer and more tolerant society.

Today, Brexit has given permission to a new and ugly wave of anti-immigrant sentiment; hate crime directed at migrants has increased ever since the Referendum took place. The Covid-19 pandemic means we are confronted by a world which has become increasingly insecure, not just for the exploited and oppressed, but even for those with money and power. It has made all of us feel more vulnerable, and has revealed the bare bones of inequality, illustrated by the pandemic's disproportionate impact on migrant communities.

How we tackle the fears that give voice to prejudice and how as a society we can navigate a way to a less unequal and more tolerant world goes to the heart of what this book is about. And it shows just how much migration enriches a society. Something we'd be wise to never forget.

For All Our Futures

Introduction to Debates about the Zeitgeist with the Second Generation

Miriam David with Merilyn Moos

Introduction to our rationale as second generation:

Exploring our personal identities and political actions became an urgent question as the twenty-first century was about to enter its third decade. As many social and psycho-geriatricians acknowledge, this exploration of family history and its implications for our lives today is a common issue for people of our age and stage of life. Witness also the popularity of new websites such as Ancestry.com and the British National Archives at Kew (KNA) (which were freely available during the first lockdown of the Covid-19 pandemic) and television programmes about family origins such as Who do you think you are?

We are now in our seventies and the question has an added piquancy, because we are not just ageing members of British society. Our particular heritage is as British children of refugees from continental Europe. A parent or parents fled Nazism and the antisemitism entwined within its specific ideology more than eighty years ago. Without Nazism and Hitler, our parents might never have met, and/or produced the children and adults we have become. We want to explore how growing up with these continental European parents affected our consciousness and personal and political experiences.

It has been difficult to contemplate looking back on our families' pasts and their impacts and this may explain why it has taken us until so late in life. Merilyn, however, had already published first a novel loosely based on her mother, a biography of her father and a carefully researched volume on anti-Nazi Germans (Moos, 2010; 2014; 2020). She has also carried out an in-depth study of the second generation through the experiences of some British children of refugees from Nazism (Moos, 2015). When Merilyn was interviewing these people, she found that they told her about their parents, not about themselves and their experiences. This was a lacuna she wished to remedy.

This study is also important at this stage of our lives because personal experience and knowledge of the experiences of fascism and Nazism will soon be lost. The first generation has mainly passed away, although there have been many individual accounts and some excellent books written by their daughters, women of the second generation (Karpf, 1997; Appignanesi, 1999; Hoffman, 2005; Saraga, 2019). Moreover, this is highly topical because we are not the only generation who have experienced having parents who are refugees, exiles, emigres, asylum seekers or migrants. Today, millions of people have been and are migrating from their countries of origin and seeking refuge from persecution, asylum or economic sustenance. In the UK, today about a quarter to a third of people born recently have at least one foreign born parent. There are more similarities with the 'new Britons' than are first apparent: many of their parents, even if not actually persecuted, would not have chosen to leave their own countries, to become dislocated, but did so for reasons of economic and/or political need.

Complex legacies and the contemporary zeitgeist:

The celebrations for seventy-five years since the Second World War ended in Europe on 8 May 2020 – Victory in Europe (VE) Day – reminded us that many people of our generation share similar backgrounds. Efforts to defeat Nazism and fascism implicated the whole of British society, along with other European countries and indeed nations around the globe as the war did not finally end until Victory in Japan (VJ) Day on 15 August 1945. It is asserted that we are 'all in it together' but we argue that there are differences in the legacies of the war. These are between those of us as the children of émigrés, exiles or refugees and the children of our generation whose parents' and grandparents' major contribution was to serve in the war.

As we are second generation, we want to tease out some of the specificities of the legacies for us. We argue that we have been involved at some deep political and psychological level, given discrimination and persecution. There is a large literature about the long-term influences, and what has sometimes been called intergenerational trauma (DeAngelis, 2019; Goldenberg, 1996). There is also a large literature about both first and second generation, but there are very few personal and political reflections.

Does our heritage as second generation have any particular inflection seventy-five years on, in a more politically febrile and charged world of globalization: what we term the current zeitgeist? Puzzling about our political legacy as well as our personal heritage is something to be disentangled. To what extent do our particular feminist and socialist politics shine a light on who we now are? Does it differ from those of our generation who have no anti-Nazi and/or Jewish heritage? By feminism, we mean a politics that foregrounds not simply social equality but relations with race, sex and gender. Nira Yuval-Davis and Miriam David wrote recently that, '...[as] two feminist social scientists, [we] address the question of antisemitism as intersectionally embedded in other forms of racisms. Intersectional analysis examines the ways *different social divisions constitute and shape each other in specific historical, locational and personal contexts* (Yuval-Davis and David, 2020).'

We, Merilyn and Miriam, share a background as second generation or daughters of refugees and hold similar politics today with commitments to gender and social equality, human rights and anti-racism as the basis of social transformation. We are also both professional educators and social scientists. But there are many differences: Merilyn brought up with what could be called 'a tyranny of secrets' and Miriam with a self-conscious knowledge of being a Jecke – someone of German Jewish background, with all the moral rectitude that this might entail.

We decided to discuss these questions about 'the interrelationship between the personal and political in an increasingly nationalistic and racist zeitgeist' with others of similar circumstances or continental backgrounds. We chose to find most of our potential participants through the Association of Jewish Refugees (AJR), which had also linked with the second-generation network. The AJR was a loose knit group formed during the Second World War to give support to incoming refugees and it has continued since then to provide a supportive network (Grenville, 2010).

We wrote a deliberate provocation for the AJR monthly journal entitled 'An Invitation to Debate the Zeitgeist': 'We write as two daughters of refugees from Nazi Germany. We understand ourselves to be part of the "second generation" (broadly defined) and are exploring how we see this as affecting our lives, both positively and negatively. How does it tie in with our commitment to equality, human rights, anti-racism and support for refugees?' (David and Moos, 2019, p.20).

We also provided thumbnail sketches of ourselves and a hint at how we had shied away from delving into the details of our pasts before, given that 'we have both had very busy professional and personal lives, and reflecting upon diverse influences was never top of the agenda. We were also brought up not to reflect or talk about the past, but to become good English women who fitted in. Talking about what happened to our families before, and during the war, was largely taboo within our families...To talk of the past would have been terrifying.'

We concluded by inviting others to tell us about their stories and whether they share with us, given that we had recently acquired German passports in response to the Brexit debates, a feeling of 'being distinct' or being 'othered'. We also sent a copy of our AJR essay to a range of feminist and socialist friends whom we knew to have a similar continental background. We hoped to have a spread of diverse men and women, and we reached out to others with that intention. We wanted to provide a safe space for discussion of these sensitive and difficult questions. This was especially given the rising tensions about fascism and antisemitism nationally and globally, what we consider the zeitgeist.

This is also relevant and topical for other groups of children of migrants and refugees from around the world. The debate about Brexit from about 2015 sparked concern not only in the UK but other countries of the EU, especially France, Germany and Ireland and raised issues of the nature of citizenship, national identity and belonging: to a country and particular social group (Yuval-Davis, 2011). The avenue to reclaim citizenship in Germany for the victims of Nazism and persecution was made available, after the end of the war, from 1949, but there were restrictions and hesitations which limited take up until the twenty-first century when the descendants of German fathers began the process of reclamation. It was only opened up for descendants of German mothers more recently. Ireland also offered this possibility for reclaiming citizenship for the children of those people who left on economic grounds in the last decade. Very recently, Austria has begun to allow citizenship applications.

The contemporary zeitgeist and being second generation:

We had no clear definition of the zeitgeist but saw it as encompassing current dominant discourse on the many issues of the day. Brexit, as it commonly became known from 2016 referendum, was crucial. As the political debate ground on, in the UK Parliament, the desire to leave the European Union (EU) and 'take back control' of British political institutions became more divisive and insistent. Debates about feelings of belonging to particular communities, whether class, social or religious, ethnicity or race and the obverse, feelings of being 'othered' became contentious. The question of universality versus uniqueness had manifold distinctions for us.

In December 2019, the election of a third Conservative government (although the first to hold a majority since 1997) led by Prime Minister Boris Johnson had given a high profile to the issue of 'Britishness' and therefore of 'non-Britishness' through 'Get Brexit Done'. The racist policy of a 'hostile environment' towards refugees, with many immigrants especially from Commonwealth countries, was only one of its many by-products, a shift in discourse likely to concern many of our contributors. A growing theme in the twenty-first century was of a racialised political discourse. Ironically, we decided on highlighting the zeitgeist before the Covid-19 pandemic which has brought to the fore the wholesale cruelty of a neo-liberal and racist perspective, including its effects on the Black, Asian and Minority Ethnic (BAME) communities and many women especially through domestic abuse, the growth of the hard right with their emphasis on 'it's all the immigrants' fault'. This is now called the 'culture wars.'

This period has also been dominated by schisms in the UK Labour party, which have deeply affected some of our contributors. This centres on attitudes to antisemitism, highlighted by investigations into the handling of antisemitism which became over-heated during Jeremy Corbyn's leadership from 2016-2020, and even more contentious under Sir Keir Starmer's leadership from April 2020. All of us, as contributors, were exercised by the possibility of the increasing acceptability of antisemitism generally and its uses and possible abuses within the

Labour Party, where it was not always linked with wider policies about discrimination and racism. How to define antisemitism has become something of a major international political debate.

From the beginning of the twenty-first century there had been growing international discussions about genocide prevention and questions of race, ethnicity and anti-racism, alongside antisemitism. The notion of the Holocaust, as a specifically Jewish issue, had only begun to gain traction in the last two to three decades of the twentieth century. Many of our contributors, including ourselves, mention that the term Holocaust was not known to their parents and they talked about the war, or Hitler, as the leader of Nazism. Initially, from the 1990s there was an international Holocaust Memorial Day on the day that the concentration camp Auschwitz was liberated. Then the International Holocaust Remembrance Alliance (IHRA) was founded over twenty years ago with the overarching aim to strengthen, advance and promote Holocaust education, research and remembrance, and to develop global initiatives for genocide prevention.

At the end of 2016, the IHRA adopted a new working definition of antisemitism, which included many new examples of what it might constitute. This was written by the jurist Kenneth Stern, a prominent Zionist and it included some highly debatable political issues about Israel and Zionism. Stern, however, has argued that the examples were not intended to limit freedom of speech and debate and has been unhappy about its wider application (Stern, 2019). The issue of antisemitism, whether on the left or the right, has become exceptionally contentious in the second decade of the twenty-first century. The definition of antisemitism has been distorted by the development of IHRA, especially over previous forms of discrimination or anti-Jewish prejudice, and tropes about Jews.

We wanted our contributors to address the present zeitgeist partly because we did not want them only to focus on their pasts. This was partly because we were interested in how far being the child of parents who had fled because of – fascist – politics affected the contributors' political leanings and partly because in a period of political upheaval, it was interesting to consider how far there is or is not a specificity to the political attitudes of the second generation. Indeed, though here we only have a very small number of the second generation, is the use of the term second generation misleading in its suggestion of shared meanings and discourse?

The design of our study in the changing context of the Covid-19 pandemic:

Our original intention had been to use face-to-face group discussions to start the process of writing our life stories. Such biographical writing has taken off as a form of expression in both academic feminist and popular literature. Both because of people's tentativeness about this approach given our complex personal legacies, and with the onset of the Covid-19 pandemic and lockdown in March 2020, we, Merilyn and Miriam, decided that we needed to use a modified form of interview questions for the task of reflexive writing. We were borrowing from various studies with which we were familiar (Oakley, 2000; Wengraf, 2001).

We drew up a checklist of questions (see Appendix 1) for an immediate writing strategy, asking contributors to address the issues we had raised in an essay of at least 3000 words. We wrote: 'As we are now in the later stages of our lives – 60s-80s – we want to look back, as women (and some men) – as socialists, anti-racists and feminists on how we got to be who we now are personally and professionally. *We suspect that our positioning is not typical.*'

We asked each contributor to think about who we are and where we are from. We were not prescriptive, but we hoped each would consider first who their parents were, and where they were from, in terms of the countries of continental Europe and whether they considered themselves emigres, in exile or refugees from Nazism. We were also interested in the process that made their parents flee from or leave continental Europe. We assumed that all of our parents had arrived in the UK before the outbreak of the Second World War. We were also interested in their experiences on arrival, and during the war, such as internment as enemy aliens. Second, we wanted to know about where we grew up: London or the provinces and how we felt about growing up with such parents, and what they told us when about their own experiences of growing up on the continent. Third, we were also interested in how our parents' values and views influenced who we became: anti-fascist, anti-racist, atheist or secular, Jewish and/or Zionist, socialist and feminist. Fourth, we also wondered about our parents' own relationships and the implications for having children. We were curious about whether some of us were only children, or, on the other hand, had siblings and how that affected how we memorialized our family backgrounds. Fifth, we wondered about how our backgrounds affected our present-day adult relationships: marriage and divorce, having children and grandchildren: similarities and differences. Finally, we were interested in our political and professional adult lives - the complex circuits and changes. We were particularly intrigued about how our present-day political concerns had drawn from our backgrounds and led us to delve into our pasts to reclaim our heritage, and commitment to fighting fascism and racism, and for human rights.

What has helped bring the collection to fruition has been the time, space and opportunity provided by the Government's confused and confusing responses to the Covid-19 pandemic. Its policies on self-isolating, shielding, social isolation and lockdown especially for our group of elderly and potentially vulnerable people, have provided a more conducive and perhaps appropriate context. First, being forced to stay at home and not have physical contact with others outside the immediate household has given some more time for contemplation, as well as more time for others for anxiety and worries. How this affects people living alone, rather than with other members of a family may be different, heightening isolation and difficulties in some, and in others a welcome chance for tidying and organizing. Second, it has enabled some of our contributors to write free from the usual constraints of regular face-to-face meetings and the quotidian buzz of life.

Perhaps this new context has provided in many cases for socially and physically distant discussions, which may feel safer than the usual face-to-face meetings. One of our contributors Charlotte Williams, a psychotherapist, says that this is consistent with the phenomenon of 'disinhibition' that therapists, in particular, have to be conversant with when doing online therapy. Such digital discussions, mainly through email and occasionally digital forms using video or zoom meetings, allow for more of an element of control and the ability to pace the discussion. These may be helpful for both physical and social distancing from others and providing the ability for this to be indeed seen as a 'project of the mind'. And yet this 'project of the mind' can also lead to enhanced paranoia or the ability to test out ideas in the safety of convivial company. This new and possibly enduring new situation, often discussed as 'the new normal', has given rise to new ways of reflecting upon our circumstances. But we must note that the apocalyptic nature of the pandemic has also produced panic and fear in others, especially those living alone and a decision not to open up in these frightening and potentially endless times.

Communalities and differences in our continental European backgrounds:

We are twelve contributors with shared parental backgrounds in continental Europe and our age cohort of all being in our early to mid-seventies. We are eleven women, with one man:

one of us women, has a very strong anti-Nazi background and no Jewish affiliation. The idea of an anti-Nazi background is varied in relation to the countries of origin of our parents, with Austria and Germany being the key, but with some parents from Czechoslovakia, Latvia and Poland. We are including three poems written by Sophie Herxheimer as they illustrate clearly and cogently how we experienced our continental backgrounds whilst we were growing up (Appendix 2). Sophie also has a continental European background and her collection of poems entitled *Velkom to Inklandt* are a response to her grandmother's experience of her life in England as a refugee and wife. She is also a cousin of Janet Leifer, one of our contributors. The poems show how the language we grew up with was often flavoured with curious grammar and expressive feelings, from a humorous perspective! This was an aspect of our difference from others we were growing up amongst where it was not always so funny. It was often mocked or ridiculed, as were our funny foreign names. We all write about this kind of background, and the continental or German food which we so loved, such as sauerkraut and frankfurters.

Some people of the first generation were also keen to be involved. One now aged 101, wrote a short letter essay for us, and referred us to his autobiography about his life as an Austrian Jewish refugee from Nazism (Sanders, 2010). We include Eric Sanders' letter essay as he deliberately engaged with the idea of the zeitgeist, and moreover, the debates about antisemitism within the Labour party. He offers a perspective of a now very elderly left-wing activist with an anti-Nazi background (see Appendix 3).

Several of us have little or no consciousness of being Jewish, whilst others are steeped in meanings of being Jewish, whether by religion or culturally, and its fundamental contestation and argumentativeness, what Alice Bondi calls 'jousting'. The question of Jewish logic and argument is indeed a key issue in some of the accounts, with its relation to a politics about antisemitism, racism and the general treatment of refugees. There is also the issue of whether being Jewish is inevitably associated with Israel and the question of it as a state, or at least a Zionist political ideology. These are inevitably nuanced and highly debatable sensitive questions.

Some of us are also from so-called 'mixed marriages' of our parents, with only one parent escaping Nazism: two with fathers (Alice and Miriam) and two with mothers (Sybil Gilbert and Clare Ungerson). Mixed marriage is also a double entendre and Alice's mother was from a Christian background whereas Miriam's was from Russian Jewish background. Sybil's and Clare's fathers were also from Russian Jewish families. This also raises the question of how far our collectively being second generation is more important than parental national differences. Whether or not we have siblings with whom to share and debate our stories is also interestingly varied with two large families (Alice and Ines) and mostly middle range or one other sibling.

But we do have, significantly, five *only* children: Merilyn, Clare, Sybil, Janet and Gaby Weiner. Gaby found out, very late in life when she came to search for her family origins that she had half-siblings whereas Irena had been brought up with the deep knowledge of her three half siblings and what had happened to them. Merilyn also found an 'adopted' sister who was her cousin, but whose mother was – and is – unmentionable. These issues of 'family secrets' are a key thread through the stories and are, inevitably, important to how we construct ourselves and our identities. They may reveal issues of shame and guilt. For example, in discussing the question with Peter Crome, he told us that he had found out, late in his father's life, that an elder brother was not a full brother, but a half-brother. Miriam found out, around the time of her divorce in the 1990s, that her German Jewish great-aunt Klara had been divorced and had a child who had died very young, a fact that had never been mentioned during her childhood.

Meanings and Significance of Being Second Generation

Interestingly, the twelve of us are not all 'technically' second generation, in the sense in which we, Merilyn and Miriam, had tried to express it. This shows how difficult it is to bring together people with fully shared backgrounds from a dramatic period of war, persecution, upheaval and turbulence. We were not all born in the UK, although we were brought up here. In particular, Peter Crome, the son of two refugees, was born at the end of the Second World War in Italy, as his 'naturalized British' father was a doctor serving in the British army. He came to live in London shortly after his birth. Ines Newman, the daughter of two émigrés from Austria and Germany, who had lived in Egypt from the 1930s and throughout the Second World War, was born in Egypt. She only came to live in Britain when she was 18 months old, in 1949. She was brought up in Orpington, south of London. Ines cannot claim to be the daughter of refugees although they were clearly from Jewish backgrounds in continental Europe. She has recently published a book about her maternal grandfather who *was* a refugee to Britain, using diaries that he wrote during the war (Newman, 2020). These nuanced differences do not detract from our similarities in how we were brought up and now view the zeitgeist broadly speaking.

Irena Fick, daughter of two passionate anti-Nazi Germans, was born in London at the end of the war, but her parents, as exiles, decided to return to Germany when she was three. So, most of Irena's upbringing was in Germany, and she only returned to London, as a young woman. She is clearly second generation in our sense. The rest of us share a similarity with

Irena in being born in Britain, but there are many differences. Only four others of us were born in London: Clare and Gaby in 1944, Janet in 1945 and Charlotte, the youngest of our group in 1950. These four were all brought up in London, and interestingly the two latter in south London, near to Peter, and the two former in central or north London near to Irena.

The other five of us were born and brought up in different towns in England: Merilyn was born in Oxford in 1944, Maggie Gravelle was born in Sheffield in 1945, Miriam was born in Keighley in 1945, Sybil Gilbert in Birmingham in 1948 and Alice was born in 1949 in Cambridge. Most of Merilyn's upbringing was in Durham, whereas Maggie moved from Sheffield to Coulsdon in south London as a youngster, and Alice's parents moved to Surrey when she was five. So, movement and upheaval were characteristics of our group too. Equally interestingly, the majority of us have migrated to living in London. Only Alice, Clare and Sybil have their main homes outside London.

How we were brought up was also very diverse: whether we were brought up as atheists or agnostics or as secular, culturally or religiously Jewish. We were all brought up knowing about our continental backgrounds, but that is about all that was shared. This was seen as important to all of us and is mentioned in all the stories, inflected as it is with a broad political critique from a socialist perspective. Irena and Merilyn were brought up as committed atheists and communists/socialists, whereas others had a more complex political and cultural background. Peter was also brought up with knowledge of his parents having been communists (and Jews). Merilyn's parents rejected their Jewish background, whilst it was of some cultural but secular significance to Clare, Maggie, Sybil and Alice, giving them some sense of being from a Jewish background. Only Gaby, Miriam, Janet and Charlotte had any Jewish education and knowledge of Judaism. Much of this was inflected with a left or socialist political commitment.

An important aspect of how we were brought up was a focus on being critical, argumentative and opinionated. This shines through many of the accounts. As already mentioned, it is what Alice refers to as jousting with her father and Miriam feels similarly about its importance in her family. Merilyn and Peter also imply its importance in their families. Nevertheless, there are clear differences between us in terms of family life, with class background feeling different in the stories. Clare, Maggie and Ines came from families that were comfortable to wealthy in Germany before the war, and this shines through their stories, including the feelings about settling down in the UK after the war. It also raises the question of how far social class has been important to us across our lives.

Who we are now: socialists and/or feminists:

There is also the question of the kinds of people we have become, from these diverse backgrounds. We are also interestingly diverse in our own social and sexual relationships, with a mention of sexuality, questions of marriage or not, divorce, remarriage and step-parenting are also a key to some of the accounts. Whether or not we have tried to create our own families out of these psychologically tumultuous events is also varied. Some of us mention not having children as relevant, whereas others mention the relevance of being a parent and relations with our children politically as well as socially. Clearly being a Jewish mother is of some importance to those of us who are, with all its implied 'controlling' connotations.

We are all university- or college-educated and mainly come from highly educated middle-class backgrounds (although one or two are from working class backgrounds). Many of us mention that our parents were highly educated too and that they went to university or higher education. This makes us a rather atypical group, although our parental education may be of some significance in our parents having the personal and/or political wherewithal to escape or flee from Nazism. Perhaps more importantly our professions are highly relevant: we are virtually all educators, involved in further or higher education with a policy, political and social scientific emphasis. Some of us combine this with forms of activism and therapy, whereas others are lawyers and librarians. All of us mention our ongoing political concerns and wishes to transform the world in some way. It is this focus on social and political transformations that are important to us and the ways in which we now construct and deconstruct our stories to make sense of the past and its implications for the future.

Moving into the individual life stories

In sum, all of us contributors to this collection had at least one parent who escaped Nazism, though for a range of reasons. Many of us call ourselves second generation but this is a term that is not always accepted and has only slowly become of significance as we shall see. It can, for instance, be seen to suggest that we are 'second-class' citizens or 'second' i.e. inferior to the 'first' generation, our parents. Sometimes we are referred to as the children of exiles, refugees or even of aliens. The term alien is no longer in common legal usage in the UK to refer to foreigners, but it was from the late nineteenth century through to the 1960s. (Interestingly it is still the legal term in the USA and Miriam's son, living in the USA, was, at the time of writing, officially a 'resident alien' as he was not yet a US citizen.) This issue appears in many of the chapters. Encouraging the contributors to put themselves centre stage and to write about their parents only in terms of how they had been affected by them was both difficult and intriguing.

One of the recurrent themes in these essays is how silent our parents were about their own pasts and that of their families, though this was not always the case. These pasts were too often peopled by members of family who had been left behind and murdered, and filled by a sea of tears, shed and unshed, of our parents. As children and youngish adults, we often knew little or nothing about the lives of the parents before they came to the UK, never mind our grandparents or other kin. Thomas Harding (2014; 2015) and Phillippe Sands (2017; 2020) as well as Merilyn (Moos, 2020) have now recuperated a great deal of their families and their histories under Nazism, and this provides an important context for our essays, too.

Some of us were brought up with ghosts and many of us felt frightened to go into an emotional space that our parents often did not wish us to enter. For many of the contributors, there was a profound reluctance to find out about the family past. Indeed, as some of the articles reveal, there is reluctance, even fear, about knowing. It is as if we were conjuring up an unbearable emotional terror. This is best avoided. It is no fun to discover what happened to our past families, whether they died as a result of antisemitism, or fell in the war. Moreover, what right did we have? But the issue of how children of refugees see themselves in the country their parents settled in is highly topical for a combination of overlapping reasons. Some want or have succeeded in living here, though some millions of migrants do not have the right of residence. This is very familiar to us.

Our parents, with only a few exceptions, had a struggle to gain British nationality. Many were interned in 1940, as enemy aliens (in some cases cheek by jowl with Nazis). How far this was a result of a war mentality, how far a product of antisemitism is a moot point, which is addressed elsewhere here in some of the chapters. But whatever the causes, our parents often wished to remain invisible and not to talk to us, their children, of their pasts. They wanted us to be assimilated or at very least integrated: *A very Englishman* resonates (Uhlman, 1960). They meant the best for us. Of course, there are differences with today's refugees and immigrants, although racism has far from gone away. Many of the contributors write about how important it is to them to be anti-racists. We feel an affinity with other refugees whose parents arrived here after ours.

It is not just anti-racism and discrimination that concern us. Many of the contributors feel in very different forms that they wanted to make this country a better place. Here we have a wide range of activists of very different sorts from anti-racist and feminist education to political and feminist projects. Given our pasts this is not a surprise though we should not assume that we can reduce these commitments to our parents' pasts. We now move on to present our twelve stories, starting first with Merilyn and Miriam. We then present the stories in alphabetical order of the authors' surnames as we do not want to prioritise any one more than another: Alice Bondi, Peter Crome, Irena Fick, Sybil Gilbert, Maggie Gravelle, Janet Leifer, Ines Newman, Clare Ungerson, Gaby Weiner and Charlotte Williams (née Prager). Each of us gives a nuanced voice to our personal experience and consequent understandings and political activities: quite how have we been impacted by histories of persecution and flight?

Chapter 2   Memories not rooted in the soil

Merilyn Moos

It was not till I was in my early sixties that I became second generation. Of course, I knew my parents were refugees. This was a point of pride. They had been active anti-Nazis who had fled for their lives after the Reichstag fire in February 1933, one month after Hitler became Chancellor. My father had been a leading member of the left-wing agit-prop movement which the Nazis detested. This provided them with a wonderful cover story as to why they had to flee. Unlike so many refugees who were forced out in the later 1930s because of antisemitism, my parents fled as a result of principle and politics.

But where were my grandparents or any other relation? I realised when very little that that asking questions about this was emotionally dangerous. My parents never mentioned the 'Holocaust' or hinted that their families had been murdered as Jews. It was all far too painful for them. I remember once, when little, somehow seeing a photo album and pointing to a picture: 'Who is he', I asked? My father snatched the album out of my hands and stormed out of the room. I was terrified. The few answers I did get, even to my young ears, sounded made-up; I learnt very young not to ask questions about the past. Dark secrets pressed hard down on me but what they were, I knew not. Even as a child, I felt death as a presence, evidence as to how transitory and ephemeral life was, a feeling I have never been able to shed.

As with many silences, my parents' inability to talk about their pasts bled into an inability to talk about almost anything. Such silence creates deep lacunae. Most families share experiences and memories, thereby creating solidarity which gives the child a sense of security. But I did not feel secure. I learnt young that I could never depend on anybody. Indeed, I was not sure how keen I was on being alive at all.

My parents too I suspect found it difficult to accept that I was alive in a foreign land when those they had cherished in the land of their birth had almost all been killed. The people who really mattered to them had lived and died in another land that I, their child, knew nothing of. What right did I have to be alive?

Yet my parents' delusions and paranoia had very real roots. My father had been hunted by the Nazis and only escaped by walking across Germany from Berlin to France, dodging the law as he went. Once in Britain, he had had his right to remain repeatedly questioned. My mother had been briefly sent to an early camp during the Nazi roundup after the Reichstag fire. On her visit to the USSR, she only just escaped with her life; after the war, she feared the long arm of the Soviet secret police far more than any Nazi relics. In Britain, at the beginning of the period of internment, she was first imprisoned in Holloway prison as a possible spy, then sent on to the Isle of Man.

They had reason to feel that the world was out to get them. My father used to hide behind a curtain convinced the house was being watched. (Was it?) The phone was covered with cushions to prevent the secret police from one nation or another from listening in. (Did they?) They concealed any vaguely left-wing book or periodical in brown paper so only when I cleared their shelves decades later, did I discover what gems lay beneath. (Once, when still 'at home', mistakenly believing I was unseen, I pulled one out, only to be told sternly by my mother that I must never touch their books again.) They had five locks on the front door. They even locked the internal doors because one never knows. The outside world was filled by enemies. Nobody could be trusted. They knew almost nobody and did not appear to even have university friends. When I brought home my first serious and left-wing boyfriend, my mother informed me the only reason he went out with me was to spy on them.

I was 'infected' by my parents' terror. They were going to die. I expected from day to day that when I came home from school, that they would be dead. I would knock frantically on the front door, always deeply relieved when it was opened. (Of course, I could not be trusted with a key.) I've never completely lost the sense that anybody close to me is going to die. (This fear is especially oppressive during the present COVID pandemic!) If a friend is late, I fear they are dead. I am not alone in this. A close friend from a similar background fears I am dead if I don't answer the phone. We live with death dripping dread into our ears.

My parents' terror that I would not survive fed into the way I behaved towards my son. Knowingly doing the opposite to them, I insisted he had an extremely active life and encouraged his many friendships but was profoundly terrified that he was dead every time he was home late, which he usually was.

My parents even hid their politics from me. To his dying day, my father denied he had ever belonged to the Communist Party. Untrue. He had been a minor but significant figure in the German Communist Party (KPD) and a leading anti-Nazi in Berlin in the early 1930s. I was left to discover the reality from MI5 files in my 60s! (My father left the KPD in 1937, from the left, and I suspect, never forgave himself for his political mistakes. I learnt very young that Stalinism was a bad thing.) When I dared once ask my mother why she had been in the USSR, I made the mistake of believing her answer.

Yet my parents' politics had some very real advantages. I absorbed a rebelliousness. In large part, this was from my mother, who refused to wear a wedding ring, a hat or gloves in public places, all unheard of in deeply conservative 1950s Durham, far removed from the cosmopolitanism of London or, indeed, early 1930s Berlin. I admired her for all this and somehow absorbed a sense that women did not have to conform to the conventional rules. Long before the 'women's movement' and after, I ignored gendered conventions

Little did I know quite how unconventional her life had been! I was only to discover almost by accident about ten years ago that the real reason for her trip to the USSR, four years after marrying my father in Berlin, was to join her Irish CP lover in Moscow. Here, it appears, she may well have gone through a civil marriage ceremony. Hounded by the Soviet secret police, she somehow escaped and after some years, went back to living with my father, but her lover was to die in the gulag.

The stuffiness and conservatism of Durham did not suit my fiery mother. She became dispirited and remote, spending most days locked away in the bedroom, writing incessantly. But despite her not conforming to the current gendered stereotypes, neither in her writing nor when I spoke to her of it, did she ever express sympathy for feminism. My mother liked men a lot and did not really believe in sisterhood.

My parents' politics seeped into the home in other ways. I loved it when my father wound up the gramophone and on special occasions, out poured Lotte Lenya (in German) or Louis Armstrong, one of the few households in Durham, I guess, to listen regularly to black jazz (though never to Paul Robeson). And, though in silence, I absorbed ideas as my intellectual parents chatted carefully over our meals. They provided me with much radical European literature (mostly in English) from their collection which I read my way through, not aware of how unusual this was.

But for me, becoming left-wing was in itself a form of rebellion. My parents did not want me to become a left-wing activist. They were terrified, with a strong element of paranoia, of the possibility of State repression. My father forbade me from supporting CND, a mass movement back then. I was not allowed out and certainly not to political events. My parents had to protect me, their only natural child, from being killed, molested, imprisoned or discriminated against. I was brought up in an atmosphere of oppressive paranoia, from which I longed to escape from an early age. I hated how claustrophobic and frightening 'home' was.

In addition, in my mid-teens, my father, for reasons I can only speculate about, also became a tad over-possessive towards me. It was another reason for me to flee home. I did not forgive him. My need to get away from him precluded real conversations; now there is so much I would like to ask him. But the distance between us was never crossed except for a couple of invaluable moments when I was pregnant. Nor was my brilliant, underachieving mother any help: she could not brook anybody she saw as competition and, once I reached an age where I could stand up to her or, God forbid, be seen as more attractive than her, could not stand me.

It is extraordinary that I came to adopt politics so similar to my parents. But I learnt about socialism not so much from them as from the parents, in particular the fathers, of my school friends, who worked in one capacity or another in the Durham mines. Growing up in Durham was key to whom I was to become. At the grammar school, almost all the girls came from working class backgrounds. Durham after all was the 'capital' of an area where the main occupation was still connected to mining and the miners' union and the Labour Party were strong.

But I turned my back on the Labour Party. I had heard my father lambasting the post First World War German Social Democratic leader, Ebert, for selling out the brief Bavarian Soviet republic (which my father witnessed). I also was very aware of the corruption and uselessness of the local Labour politicians. I understood the limitations of left social democracy then and now. I have continued to refuse to belong to the Labour Party, though Jeremy Corby's leadership was a wonderful reminder that a different world is possible.

I went to university open to revolutionary ideas in the very period when the Cold War dominated discourse was starting to be challenged. There I first joined the Socialist Society, to the left of the Labour Club and then the neo-Trotskyist International Socialists (IS) after I encountered them on an anti-Cuban crisis demonstration!

After completing my degree at Oxford University, I was too busy to excavate the buried world of my family's pasts. I had moved to London, become an FE lecturer, a trade-union activist, the college ATTI (then NATFHE) Branch Secretary and much else besides. This was a period of hope: of a growing non-Stalinist left, of May 1968, and of the growing feminist movement. I probably spent longer organising than I did lecturing. I had loads of friends. I became involved in significant anti-racist campaigns, some of the best things I've done. Later than most women, I had a baby, though mislaying the father along the way, a consequence of multiple misunderstandings more than a feminist stand.

Another reason I did not look into the past was how I felt about my parents. I wanted nothing to do with them. This is not the place to explore the many analyses and theories about the causes for hostility between some refugee parents and their children, but I certainly am an example of such family rupture. Living in the present not in the past was what mattered to me.

Although my recollection of the exact order of events has become vague, when my, by now, elderly mother was hospitalised, I grasped the moment and seized the foolscap brown battered envelopes which, strangely, were lying on her desk, stuffed with scrunched up letters from Nazi Germany. I was in for a shock. I could not read the German (including some old German), but a loose translation provided evidence I had not anticipated: my mother's parents wanted to get out of Germany because they were – or at least were defined as being Jews. My mother had denied being Jewish. I had been brought up without any knowledge of Jewish customs, never mind religious rituals. The ghosts of the past were taking form.

The dominant discourse had also shifted. The concern about the effects of Nazism from the 1970s became increasingly – and more narrowly – defined through the 'Holocaust'; the concept of the 'second generation' had also developed currency. I had never defined myself as second generation. I was active in revolutionary politics and wanted to bring about fundamental change in present day society. My concern was not defining myself through my parents' pasts.

I was in my late fifties when I started to attend meetings of the second generation. I had always been involved in anti-racist issues and to some degree, around refugees. Some deep bell of recognition finally chimed inside me. But things did not go well. What quickly emerged was that most, though not all, of the people there, saw themselves as victims, a perspective I reject. The group did not welcome my more political approach. Although not a term that was employed, the emphasis was on how powerful and inevitable 'transferred trauma' was. I struggled on for a couple of years till there was a major falling out over attitudes to Israel. I was and am an anti-Zionist and that was that.

But a door had opened and, slowly, I researched my parents' families. It is then that being second generation took on meaning. The children of refugees from Nazism are often unlike many more recent groups of refugees where there is a sense of a 'familial' home and even of a possible return. Elders regale their children with stories of their earlier lives. There is a hope of return. But none of my family would have countenanced a return to either E. or W. Germany. But I did not feel that I belonged here either.

My disjuncture from the past had been especially acute. When the second-generation child has one British born parent, then that parent can on occasion become the story-teller about the other parent's past. Or the child gets to know an old relative, maybe even a grandparent, who somehow survived who tells them about their family. But none of this applied to me. I had grown up without family stories. I was told nothing at all about my grandparents. I did not know their names, where they lived, what they had done or, of course, how they had died. I had no soil in which to root any memories, no past to define myself through. My memories had to be constructed.

I had grown up with ghosts but finding out about who the ghosts were hurt. I visited the synagogue in Berlin to try to find out about what had happened to my mother's parents. (One died a 'natural' death, one in Theriesenstadt and my aunt was gassed in Brandenburg.) Over many painful years, I built up a family 'tree', a tree with too many spaces for the exact date of death. I discovered that my father's parents were not his parents but his 'adopted' father also died in Theriesenstadt (in especially appalling circumstances). I have not been able to trace my father's mother. The Nazis defined them all as Jewish.

Of course, Jewishness has many meanings. For my mother, Judaism was a religion: have you ever seen me in a synagogue, she would snap. My father was a committed atheist. To add further complexity, he had been enrolled in a Catholic secondary school as a Protestant. If I had ever managed to push him, I know he would have said that to end intolerance, including antisemitism, one has to organise to transform (or maybe to end) capitalism. Although their relatives had been murdered because the Nazis defined them as Jews, my parents, in a fashion popular on the left at the time, saw the Jews as failing to organize against the Nazis. (As we now recognise, many anti-Nazis were Jewish, though not always defining or organising themselves primarily as such.) Asked in my 20s, 30s or 40s if I was Jewish, I was not lying when I said no.

My parents had sought my assimilation: the language spoken at home was English (generally) as were most of my children's books and I attended a Church of England primary school and, later, a Grammar school, where I sang 'Christian' hymns along with all the other children. My parents' emphasis on assimilation was in part, I suspect, an expression of a desire to protect me from suffering any possibility of future antisemitism. They could get away with this. I was fair-haired and could easily pass as a stereotypical Aryan child. When we were in Germany in the late 1940s when I was about 5, a man rushed up to us, picked me up and delighted, threw me into the air, saying: 'Eine Deutsche madchen'. My parents seized me back. I was terrified.

But I never felt myself to be assimilated (not that I knew of this concept till a grown-up). Looking back, I see myself as an 'outsider'. There are many reasons. At my Protestant primary school, I ploughed my own, friendless furrow. I had already somehow absorbed my parents' critical edge, the only pupil to question the teachers' almost daily diet of evangelism. I did not see it as making sense. Indeed, it was their religious teaching that turned me into an early agnostic. I was condemned as 'Doubting Thomas' by my class-mates! I was also different in that the other kids had extended families: I still remember how when the teacher told us to draw our families, the other girls covered their paper with pictures of grandmothers, aunts and cousins, while all I could draw were my two parents and feel left out and bewildered.

At Durham Girls' Grammar School, I made a couple of friends (one life-long) but inviting them home, as would have been normal, was difficult: my mother served up our normal food but pumpernickel and wurst were alien foods (even spaghetti was unknown at the time in Durham) and my socialist mum was also a snob who did not want me influenced by working class adolescent friends, especially as they became increasingly interested in boys. (She need not have worried: I was a slow developer.) My father even told me I didn't want to be friends with 'them'. (Oh yes, I do!) When I was 17, he threatened one of his students, who had made the mistake of going out with me, with expulsion from Durham University where he was a lecturer if he didn't stop seeing me. I was my parents' most precious possession: my birth and existence proved the Nazis had not won. But it left me lonely, and apprehensive about men. Leaving home and 'going up' to Oxford University was a relief.

It is impossible to untangle how far my experience of being the child of refugees has been tempered by my being a woman. Till I reached puberty, my parents' Berlin-inspired beliefs in gender equality informed the way they brought me up. My father encouraged me to read copiously, develop my own ideas and instructed me on how to climb trees. As long as I was a child, I was free to roam. But once I reached puberty, all hell broke loose. Any man who dared show interest had to be driven away. No man must be allowed to remove me from him. My father told me I must never be seen with a man in public. (It would damage his reputation.) My mother screamed at me about my sluttish behaviour with men. (Sadly, her invention.) She would have loved a son who would have adored her and could have shown her off. But I was seen as a rival. I became afraid of myself.

In a way familiar amongst female war children and baby-boomers, I also lacked ambition. The head mistress in my grammar school had told us, much to my fury even at the time, that us girls could not climb to the top of the tree, but only to the top of the bush. When I went up to Oxford, women could not even have membership or vote in the union: I became involved in the campaign to get women the vote! Only 1:7 of the students at Oxford were female, mostly from public schools and hardly any were on the left. I was also accustomed to working class girls, who spoke with a North Eastern accent and in ways I still cannot quite put my finger on, approached life differently from their middle and upper class 'sisters'. I was not very close to any woman at Oxford.

I suspect I was also not an easy person to have a close relationship with. I had a low sense of self-worth and became easily anxious. I married but we separated, though I had other long relationships along the way. I squeezed in a child just before the biological clock closed down, only after I finally realised, largely thanks to my partner of the time, that children did not have to go through the years of being as terrified and lonesome as I had and that it was OK for me to have a baby. But it was a near-run thing.

Women, as second-generation literature has shown, are more likely to feel a responsibility for their psychologically ship-wrecked parents, while hating them at the same time. My mother, after the sudden death of my father, effectively blackmailed me. If I went away for even the weekend, she would kill herself. Which was indeed what she attempted to do. She also refused to answer the phone so that, always terrified she had had a fall or had yet again tried to commit suicide, I drove frantically to where she lived in Hackney. She regularly refused to open the front door. In my son's early years, I spent longer trying to look after my mother than I did looking after him. I hated her. But what was she to do? Apart from me, she had no family to speak of, had a terrible past which she refused to talk about, had virtually no real friends and was, as she wrote, a stranger in an alien land. She certainly kept me busy.

By now, my parents are long dead. My son is very grown up. I read about Nazism, examining its causes and effects. My latest book is about the German resistance to the Nazis (Moos & Cushion, 2019). So many ambiguities remain. I seized on the German state's offer to the children of those who had to flee Nazism to adopt German citizenship. But while this represents a reclaiming of a country my parents had to flee, and which removed their German citizenship, as significant for me is that I and my son are able to escape a reactionary Brexit Britain. I have never felt German. Although my first children's books were in German, and it was the language frequently used between my parents, especially when they did not want me to understand what they were saying, they must have decided to change policy: I had to be like other children. My mother, anyway, hated the Germans. I am, as a friend put it, a 'not-German'.

But I have also never felt British (and certainly not English). Faced with those endless questions about ethnic origin, if at all possible, I cross them out or tick something like 'other'. While I love my house in Islington, North London where I – and my son – have lived, when I visited and gave a talk about my mother and her family at the apartment block (now a German national monument) where my mother grew up in Charlottenburg, Berlin, I felt as near to being 'at home' as anywhere I've experienced. Now the Holocaust is paying a repeat visit, not in reality but in the imaginings of us whose parents fled the Nazis. The present COVID-19 pandemic feeds into an existential sense of threat to our being, of insecurity, uncertainty and even paranoia, the very characteristics we often absorbed.

The silence of many, even if not all, of our refugee parents, even if well meant, left us feeling a level of uncertainty about our pasts and about ourselves. It left us unable to construct a coherent story about ourselves. We absorbed a sense of almost constant dread that something terrible could happen to us or to those we loved. Such terrors, uncertainties and insecurities are now being brought back to the psychological surface of our beings by the present pandemic. This is not like a one-off emergency which, however terrible, we know will resolve in the not-too-distant future. Rather, there is a sense of a never ending and constant threat.

If, like me, you are in the highest risk group, according to some scientists, it may not be 'safe' for me to mix with others till there is an effective and extensive programme of vaccines. When this will be is at best, an unknown and, some predict, could be at least 18 months. We are in the grasp of an invisible, malign and uncontrollable force. Just as when we were children, it as if death is sneaking up on us and there is almost nothing we can do about it.

Moreover, as during the Holocaust, though there were rare – and honourable – instances of resistance, so now, there appears almost nothing we can do apart from hide. But that is also not possible. Some interaction with the outside world is essential: we need food, medicines, to see doctors or visit hospitals, we may need help to look after our pets or our homes. All such interactions are both necessary and bring dread. Being in hiding is also resonant. Many of our parents, for different reasons, felt they needed to remain invisible both before they fled and once here as refugees. They often, though not always, saw the world as a hostile place. Unlike our parents, we have little reason to feel unwelcome and the world is not out to get us, but the slippage into the foothills of paranoia is an easy one.

The joys of the external are now largely denied us. Where before, we would meet with friends or go out to do something enjoyable, whether by ourselves or with partners, family or friends, that emotional bolt hole is now slammed shut. Even going for a walk to breathe in the spring-time, is perceived in terms of risk. We are shut off from almost all the joys of the outside world and from the face-to-face support of others. We feel discombobulated, panicky, under threat even from those near-or dear- to us.

But that does not mean facing death is any easier. We who grew up with the spectre of death now feel the Covid-19 pandemic brings it even closer. People I know are writing – or rewriting – their wills, tidying up their personal papers, and having intimate conversations with their loved ones about what they want to happen if they get the virus. Do I prefer to die alone at home or die alone in hospital? Our acute awareness of the pandemic presses down on fragile sense of joy at living in the present.

This government's inept handling of the pandemic, fuelled by their neo-liberal agenda, Europhobia and a good dose of incompetence, borders on corporate manslaughter. The world-wide spread of the virus has resulted to a large degree from the increasingly rapacious domination of world-wide capitalism's drive for profits. The increasingly influential radical right's ideology that humankind can control nature and do with it as it wants, is shown up in all its lethal falsity. My exclusion – in effect – from civil society is a consequence of grand politics. I find my enforced passivity difficult to bear.

The past we thought we had moved on from or come to terms with is rushing back to the surface of our beings. Our boundaries appear to be in dissolution. The grasp of the murderous past pulls us towards it, even as we struggle to be ourselves. My parents' lives were embedded in the twentieth century, profoundly influenced by the Russian Revolution, fleeing Nazism and settling in a country, which, post-war, became defined through its social democratic praxis, only, I imagine to their despair, for it to descend back to neo-liberalism. Like so many tens of millions, they did not die in the country where they had been born and never quite felt Britain to be where they belonged. Having a child here – me – brought to the fore many of their deep insecurities and uncertainties which, despite my slow accretion of 'memories', has left me always aware of not being quite at 'home' here. But at the same time, their legacy to me was to always question, to always confront the powerful and I see myself as following in their footsteps as I have struggled to create an anti-sexist, anti-racist, more equal and preferably socialist society.

Now, in my mid-seventies and sadly enduring a much too fast decline, it is time for looking backwards, for trying to understand how far being 'second generation' has framed who I became. Understanding its complex and frequently contradictory contours has enabled me to inhabit my own skin more fully. 'Historically' Jewish, my parents fled because of their anti-Nazi politics and activities. It was not easy being their child, but I am proud that I was. I reject the construction of myself as victim. I stand strong in a political tradition. I am a socialist, an internationalist and a fighter against injustice.

Chapter 3   Being the daughter of an enemy alien: is this second generation?

Miriam E. David

I have always known that my father was born in Frankfurt-am-Main, Germany, and that he came to England to escape Nazism, in the mid 1930s. I was told that he came to a professional engineering job in Manchester and it was here that he met my mother, through a Zionist organisation, in about 1937. My mother was born in Manchester, brought up in Oldham and went to Manchester University. Whether or not my father was a Jewish refugee was a question, not a certainty. In 1980, shortly after my father's death, I wanted to dedicate my book *The State, The Family and Education,* to him as a Jewish refugee. Talking to my mother about it, she said that he was not a refugee as he came to a job. I never understood the vehemence of her statement to me then. It is only now that I have come to realise its full import having finally managed to piece it together from scraps of memorabilia, long buried away. These illustrate how the British state dealt with refugees, or aliens as they were then called, and their families. As a still dutiful daughter (like Simone de Beauvoir), I changed the dedication to say: 'For my father, whose untimely death deprived me of the chance to argue about patriarchy with him'. This was published in September 1980 in Routledge's then Radical Social Policy series and it spoke to my growing feminist sensibilities, based as it was upon my teaching at the University of Bristol on women, family and social policy (David, 1980).

I have continued to agonise about what to call my father, and the Nazism of Germany that he escaped leading to the Second World War. I also still agonise about who I am, therefore, and how marginal I am to the so-called mainstream in my very being. As to whether I am 'second generation' is also a moot point, given that I am only half, although not very far back as third generation on my mother's side. My mother was also the daughter of refugees, her parents coming to the UK from Russia to escape antisemitic pogroms in the late nineteenth century. To use the legal term for a foreigner at the time, I am the granddaughter of four aliens and the daughter of an 'enemy alien'. This feels like an incredibly uncomfortable term to accept and live with, especially in the zeitgeist of the second to third decade of the twenty-first century.

The term 'alien' is no longer in common usage in the UK although perhaps it underlies all that is currently discussed about refugees or migrants from around the world. (It remains the official term for foreigners in the USA, and my son was an American 'permanent resident alien'). It also hints at the notion of a 'hostile environment' as promulgated by a previous Conservative government. How to deal with the issues of racism and sexism in the context of the Covid-19 pandemic, especially but not only in the UK, has become a central question both for the inequalities in relation to care and health workers and also for those who die from the virus. Black and Minority Ethnic (BAME) people are significantly more likely to be impacted. Given my proud commitment to fighting both patriarchy or sexism and antisemitism as an aspect of racism, the continuity with my parents' feelings and actions is coming to the fore.

The terms exile or émigré seem pretentious and inappropriate, as my father tried hard to speak English in a very down-to-earth way, even adopting a Yorkshire accent. Until very recently, I have not felt that the German and Austrian exile studies centre at the University of London had anything to do with me. I am still not sure that my father felt that he was exiled, although he might have felt he had emigrated from 'the continent' to the UK. Refugee as a term was altogether more in keeping with what my father seemed to feel about being in England and bringing up his three daughters in the small working-class town of Keighley in West Yorkshire. We were unique as there were no other Jews in the town, but we did begin to meet some when we started going regularly to the Bradford Hebrew congregation, when I was about seven or eight. Here we became very friendly with children of Austrian, Czechoslovakian and German refugees, mainly through the Hebrew classes at Sunday school or Cheder. (I remain friendly with some of them.) This was a weekly occurrence and, at first, not nearly as significant as the quotidian life in Keighley: marginality was built-in so-to-speak. I tried desperately to fit in as an ordinary girl, but well remember another girl of about seven, asking me if I was born in Jerusalem as I was Jewish!

We had few family relations to grow up with, since by the time I was able to remember, my German grandparents and great grandmother had passed away in Manchester, and my father's elder and only brother (with a daughter six months older than me) had gone to live in South Africa. My father's closest relative was an elderly (but younger than I am today) Aunty Klara who lived in a Jewish refugee old age home in Manchester. We did visit her regularly and she occasionally came to stay. She could barely speak to us as her English was poor. I was very fond of her as she seemed so sad and lonely, and a spinster, and the home she lived in so dark and dingy.

My mother's family also lived a long way away, as my grandmother had left Manchester at the end of the war, to go and live in Southend, to be near to her elder daughter, ten years my mother's senior, Aunty Bec. Uncle Maurice, twenty years mum's senior, was a pharmacist and Aunty Bec his assistant and they lived both in Chalkwell, and Plaistow, east London, where the chemist's shop was. We had regular Christmas visits to Southend when my father got a car, in the early 1950s, along what we called the 'pipping road' from London to Southend. We always visited my mother's bachelor elder brother, Uncle Jo, in London first. He travelled abroad for his work as an insurance broker and would come on regular visits bearing exotic gifts. He and Uncle Maurice were jolly and fun members of the family, whereas Aunty Bec was somewhat sad like Aunty Klara and I felt for her too: none had children.

Our family was full of distant and elderly people, and we had no close cousins in England. This was a huge contrast with my non-Jewish friends growing up in Keighley, whose families were entirely local. We did have some girl second cousins of our age who lived at the eastern most end of Yorkshire. Given transport in the late 1940s and early 1950s Hull was relatively inaccessible. Also, my father and his cousin Lotte did not get along very well. My only memory is of a simmering row about whether to go for German reparations for their grandfather's corn mill in Friedberg and a shadow hung over our relations because of it. My father took the moral high ground and did not want to have anything more to do with Germany, although he did get letters from Germany through the post on a regular basis. We did not know what they were about, nor were we allowed to ask. In 1955, my father went on a business trip to the USA, on the Saxonia, and we went to Liverpool to see him off. As part of that trip, he reconnected with many of his wider maternal family – his mother's brothers and sister and their children – whom he had not seen for 20 years. This was a very emotional event for him and so for us. We saw such relatives as precious and I have remained in touch with several of them over the years, despite the fact that many do not share my politics.

The term holocaust was barely in the lexicon, and my parents spoke of the war, and what happened during it, in hushed tones. It was only around the time that my father died in 1980 that the term holocaust came into common usage, as about the specifically Nazi holocaust on mainly Jews. The first time I recollect this was through a miniseries on television, that came out in 1978, in the USA called *Holocaust* with Meryl Streep in a debut part. The series was also heavily criticised although very informative about the outlines of what happened to two intertwined families in Berlin.

The film *Shoah* (meaning Holocaust in Hebrew) Claude Lanzman's masterpiece came out about five or six years later in the mid-1980s. It was the first major critical and personal account of eyewitnesses and participants across Europe, including countries I had not really realised were so devastated by Nazism. I will never forget the experience of sitting through about five or six hours of it at the Phoenix cinema in East Finchley and how over-whelming it was. This was shortly after I had moved to London with my then husband and two young children and a family friend also son of refugees, babysat for us. The film was a most remarkable experience, as much because almost all the footage, across many European countries was of men, rather than women. And yet, at this time, Lanzman was a protégé, and sometime lover, of Simone de Beauvoir.

Whilst I was growing up, we were never allowed to buy anything German, and shops such as C & A were barred to us because of their Nazi associations. The idea of buying a Volkswagen, for example, was absolute anathema. On the other hand, we did eat lots of German or European food, in contrast with the other children growing up around us. I remember, for example, going to the delicatessen shop along the high street in Keighley to buy pickled cucumbers and sauerkraut, after having been to collect our rations of orange juice etc near the bus station.

My father did not consider a meal 'proper' without soup, and so we had soup at almost every evening meal and on a Friday night. Meals around the dinner table, especially on Friday nights, and Saturday lunchtime, after my father had come home from working on a Saturday morning, were argumentative, heated and noisy. Politics was always included and especially knowing about local, national and international political situations. My parents insisted on discussing the news from a left or liberal perspective. *The Manchester Guardian* was a staple in our house and we always listened to the news on the home service on the wireless.

My parents got very involved in our education, with my mother being a regular attendee at the PTA of Keighley Girls' Grammar School (KGGS) and my father becoming the chair of the Bradford Hebrew Congregation's education committee. One year, my mother got my father to give a talk to the PTA, and I remember his impassioned plea against capital punishment. Our Jewish education was organised as Sunday school, which we attended regularly from about seven or so. My father took my sisters and me by car to Bradford, a journey of about ten miles, but we three sisters came home on our own by bus to Keighley station, and then another bus up the hill to Exley Head. We didn't go to synagogue on a regular weekly basis and when we went on the high holydays we went by bus. We did, though, take off all the major Jewish festivals so in an Autumn term, we could sometimes lose as many as seven school days for Rosh Hashannah, Yom Kippur, and Succot. This felt like an exclusion and separation from normal school life.

My parents were also involved with their own professional organisations, and my father was chair of Institute of Production Engineers, based in Melton Mowbray, for several years. Getting involved was a sine qua none of growing up: politically, socially and professionally. Talking about Germany and the past was rather more problematic. My father told us lots of anecdotes about his family and the food they ate, and what he had done growing up in cosmopolitan and metropolitan Frankfurt and what Jewish life was like there. We knew that his parents didn't always agree on how religious to be, with his father being a wine merchant more of a bon viveur.

My father also used to regale us with German, Latin and Hebrew aphorisms for learning things. Fairly recently, I found that Hannah Arendt used similar phrases in her collection *Men in Dark Times*. Even more recently, reviewing a book of the German and Austrian Exile Centre, one contributor used the phrase which was how my father referred to home – *Beiunskiland*. He was clearly very proud of some aspects of German culture – Heine, Schiller and music. He had learned to play the violin when he was growing up. He was disappointed in how his daughters did not have a good ear for music.

We also heard about his education first through the rich Jewish culture in Frankfurt (for example, the social democrat philosopher Erich Fromm's father was the reader in his synagogue *Unterlindau*), second at a *gymnasium* – similar to a grammar school – and then in Darmstadt for two years, studying engineering, and later two years in Berlin at the elite *Technische Hochschule*. We also were told about his friends and the networks he joined such as the Jewish rowing club in Berlin, and the socialist-Zionist groups.

On Hitler's rise to power in 1933, we learnt that my father had lost his position doing a doctorate, under a Professor Schlesinger, as academics were seen as being public servants. My father went east to a job in Neisse, in upper Silesia, then part of Prussia or greater Germany, but now in Poland. It was here that he, as a machine tool design engineer, realised that Hitler was preparing for war. He decided to leave and got a professional post at Kendall and Gent and digs in Whalley Range, Manchester. He had wanted to go to Palestine (as Schlesinger did) but was not able to afford the fees required. He also felt that Hitler made him more Jewish conscious than he had felt hitherto. Although he had been brought up in a strongly Jewish way, this did not define what and who he might become. He toyed with a range of left and liberal politics but was afraid to become too involved in criticisms of the state in either Germany or England.

There were then many no-go areas in what we were told about the war. As my mother only knew bits of Yiddish and not German, German was not spoken at home, but my father did use German phraseology. We were not expected to learn German but concentrate on more scientific subjects, although my mother had studied the humanities. I was offered a choice of German or chemistry at school for GCE 'O' levels. Given that my elder sister had chosen chemistry as a subject for GCE 'A' level and potentially for university, I chose German. I was taught by a Jewish refugee, a Viennese woman, who had converted to Christianity in the 1930s. As she was from Austria, she spoke German with a different pronunciation from my father: there were many contestations. My father saw himself as speaking '*Hoch Deutsch*'. Indeed, we learnt somewhat jokingly about the cultural snobbery of German Jews, often called Jeckes, a term meaning people who wore jackets, and were always smart and correct, including always being precise and on time. I was so imbued with this that I still feel myself to be a Jecke and am proud of it. But it has its downsides, such as being exclusive rather than inclusive.

I heard, for example, that there were tensions between my father's snobbish middle-class German Jewish family and my mother's equally snobbish but differently so, middle class family. We vaguely knew that my parents had what was jokingly called a 'mixed marriage' between two different kinds of Jews – from Germany and Russia. Both, interestingly, were very enthusiastic and competitive about education. Little did we know then though the full import for women.

We moved from Keighley to Shipley to be nearer to the orthodox Bradford Jewish community, when my younger sister had finished primary school, and I was just thirteen. This move meant that we gained more of a Jewish communal life, and yet we were more of a distance from our former friendships and the local school community. This felt like another form of marginality for me. I still feel half in and half out of any of the organisations I belong to. For instance, at the event for the fiftieth anniversary of women's liberation held in Oxford I wasn't sure that I really belonged. Should I really have been there then and now?

More important, I often wanted to know more about my father's friends and political activities in Germany and felt he wouldn't talk. He seemed rather 'buttoned up' or closed down. He was keen for us to debate and argue with him and so I continued to badger about this, on occasion. I well remember one Friday night dinner table conversation, when I begged my father to say more. My mother urged me to stop, but given his expectations of me, I persisted. Finally, my father broke down in tears about some of his friends who were very left-wing, possibly communists, and had left Berlin for Russia where they had perished. I can still feel his hurt and upset.

Although we knew that my father had been interned, with his father, and his elder brother, in Huyton, Liverpool and later on the Isle of Man, early on in the war, we were told very little about it. We learnt about some of the famous people who were also interned – musicians such as Rawicz and Landauer, the Amadeus string quartet and painters. He told us how it was a hive of educational activities, including learning about bee-keeping and university studies. It was a well-known fact to us as we were growing up, but never fully discussed or explicated. My parents did not dwell on its more difficult and painful downsides. Rather, we often discussed socialist politics and knew that Huyton was Harold Wilson's constituency, first as a Labour MP from 1950 and later as leader of the Labour party in 1963 and Labour Prime Minister from 1964-70 and 1974-76. He remained the MP for Huyton until 1983.

Indeed, growing up I felt that the one key aspect of my marginality being Jewish was entirely a family and personal affair whereas my public life was at school and in friendships.

Talking publicly about antisemitism was not seen to be wise, as it might invoke exactly what was taboo. The recent and constant noise about antisemitism and especially in the Labour Party whilst Jeremy Corbyn was leader therefore is very hurtful to me as it contradicts my very sense of what is proper and appropriate.

We always had lovely summer holidays first in the British Isles, and I have found the postcards that my father sent Aunty Klara to prove it. From when I became ten, we began to go on continental holidays, first to Noordwijk, The Netherlands, and later to Switzerland, Italy and France. Returning one summer, I remember my father's complaint in a small hotel in Dover about the poor breakfast service compared with being on the continent. The reply was 'You are not on the continent now'. It reinforced my growing sense of being cosmopolitan rather than local, or rather the insularity of the English.

We never went to Germany as children, and my father also boycotted Spain because of General Franco and the fascism there. One summer, as a young adult, I went to Pamplona with a boyfriend, but never told my parents. In 1970, my father grew angry about the rightward tendencies in France. He decided that he would like to go and visit Germany with my mother. My younger sister, Anne and I were invited a long too for a long weekend. My elder sister had married and had a small six-month-old son and so she was not invited. Anne and I flew to Zurich where my parents picked us up and we drove into Germany through the *Rheinfalls* and down the Rhine, through Cologne and into Frankfurt. We spent about three nights there, visiting Frankfurt, Friedberg (where my grandmother was born) and a spa town that I confused on the photos I took. It later turned out to be Bad Nauheim very close to Friedberg, but I placed it as Bad Homburg another slightly more distant spa town where we must have stayed. I think my confusion was because of how traumatic it was. It all felt both incredibly and emotionally very tense: my father was asked where he had learnt such good German! I now know the difference between the two spa towns as we went back to an event in 2008 to commemorate the Jews of Friedberg. We stayed in Bad Nauheim which is where Elvis Presley had lived when he was a GI, and there was a fiftieth anniversary celebration for him, at the same time as the seventieth anniversary event for the expulsion of the Jews of Friedberg. Bad Nauheim is also famous for where major international and scientific conferences have been held. When Elvis Presley popularised the song 'Wooden Heart' in 1960 my father was appalled at his German pronunciation and taught us the correct version: *Muss ich denn*!

In the later stages of my professional life, I have tried to explore aspects of my becoming a socialist-feminist and a sociologist. After my mother died in 1996 (sixteen years after my father), we also began the process of finding out more about our family backgrounds by searching through some of the many boxes and paraphernalia that we found in the house she had moved to in London, after my father had died. We divvied out the furniture, books, and mementoes on what seemed an equitable basis. I had already acquired the only piece of furniture that my father brought to England – a five-section bookcase – in which I now keep all my precious Jewish books, both religious and secular. I also took many of the German books and tried, when we first reorganised and then downsized about five years ago, to give them to the Wiener Library but they weren't sufficiently precious. I had to give them to booksellers in the hope that they would find homes, rather than go to landfill.

We also found in a locked box the Nazi passports of my father, his parents and grandmother and great aunt and began the process of searching out more information about how they had all come to England. My father, we discovered, had arrived on his twenty-eighth birthday 27 October 1936, and my grandparents, great-grandmother and great aunt on 31 July 1939, just a month before war broke out. Apart from my father's passport, because he had come before the major rise in antisemitism, all the passports had the names of Israel or Sarah between forename and surname. My grandfather was Adolf Israel David and my grandmother Clementine Sarah David. We also realised that my father had come the recognised conventional way – by train and ship – whereas my grandparents' flight was literally that. They had flown from Cologne, arriving in Manchester Ringway airport. Nevertheless, this still did not explain all the details in their passports, and I am now beginning to realise that the four relatively elderly people had perilous journeys by train and plane.

I also contacted the Association of Jewish Refugees (AJR) and got copies of the 'slips' or forms that my father and his family had filled in, which gave us far more information than we had ever known before. For me, I learnt that Aunty Klara had been married and divorced. I also found out from Aunty Klara's prayer book that she had had a son called Eugen born in 1906, who had died possibly in the Spanish flu pandemic. This divorce was a family 'secret' and probably a shameful issue. I found all of this out a few years after I went through a divorce from my first husband. He was a first- or second-generation Jewish refugee, since he was born in Hungary in January 1946. His parents immediately left Hungary, where his mother had been in hiding and his father had been in a labour camp in Russia in the later stages of the war. They came via Paris and Nice to England, arriving when Robert was three. This all led me to feel, throughout my twenty-year marriage, that Robert's suffering and his parents' survival against the odds were far more painful and traumatic than anything my family had suffered. Perhaps this kind of suffering cannot be put on the balance scales and I had done the usual female submission of deferring to my husband's family tragedies.

As a result of finding the family material, we developed family trees and I made a power-point presentation for our children and grandchildren, which I subsequently presented at the Wiener Library (Spring 2015). We had worked on a legacy project for the Jewish Cultural Centre about ten years before its demise, or amalgamation with JW3. We were encouraged by Joanna Millan, who had been one of the so-called Windermere children with a close friend of ours, Denny Muench. They had both been survivors of *Theresienstadt* (Moskovitz, 1983).

We also had found all the necessary documents, such as birth certificates and passports, in order to acquire German citizenship about four years ago. I was encouraged by two of my nephews because of looming Brexit. My son and daughter were less pressing for different reasons: Toby living in the US and Charlotte's child a tiny baby. Having a Hungarian Jewish refugee for a father also complicated their second or third generation status.

In keeping with the developments in auto/biography in the social sciences, I also developed an intellectual biography (David, 2003). I spelled out in considerable detail my family origins, but curiously, I did not concentrate on the significance of my background as the daughter of a German Jewish refugee and second generation. Nor did I do so in subsequent personal and political reflections (David, 2016a; 2016b).

I now realise why my mother so objected to calling my father a refugee, as being a refugee nowadays, still bears all the hallmarks of being stigmatised. My mother was struggling with her own identity, especially as a woman, as well as the prospect of marrying an alien. Recently, I found a tiny newspaper cutting in my parents' belongings, and in her diary for 1940, when finally looking through assorted memorabilia. There were also diaries and addresses books which included small but important details of where my father was interned in Huyton and on the Isle of Man. These tiny calling cards were in my mother's writing but in my father's address book and diary for 1940. The most important finding was the tiny newspaper cutting

with no referents as to date or type of paper:

Ranked as idiots

Since 1870 British women marrying aliens have been classed as lunatics and idiots,

said Mrs Spiller of the Women's Freedom League, yesterday. They demand a bill to

put their status right.

Clearly my mother, herself the daughter of aliens, was quite exercised about this. We had

known that my mother was interested in women's suffrage, that the Pankhursts had started

out in Manchester and that she voted as soon as she was able to (aged 21) in 1931, having

Eleanor Rathbone (as MP for the English universities) as one of her two MPs. When my mother

married my father on 22 June 1941, she lost her British nationality. We found an official letter

dated November 1941, that stated she had to pay 5 shillings to get it back. I had not thought

to find out when women were able to keep their own nationality status on marriage. Is this

yet another example of women's oppression and how I too am caught up in its very sinews,

despite all my efforts to be a feminist activist?

Even so, it does not fully spell out how being a woman in relation to the alien or refugee

status is perhaps yet another form of women's oppression, which is generally hidden from

view. Of course, my grandmother, my great-grandmother and great aunt all arriving from

Germany in late July 1939 must have had to struggle with their changing identity as women

refugees, subordinate to the male members of the household. They also had to struggle

with a new language, living alone and in financially straitened circumstances when my

grandfather, my father and his brother were interned 10 months later. The memorabilia include information on how to behave as a refugee or alien in England, especially during wartime.

The issue for my mother as a professional woman, teacher and contemplating marriage to an 'enemy alien' during the war, must have been very disconcerting. I have now discovered that there was a major feminist campaign throughout the 1930s to change the status of women who married foreigners. From the 1870 Naturalization Act, women who married aliens lost their British nationality 'being equal in status to infants, lunatics and idiots' (Baldwin 2001, p.5). Having campaigned successfully for women's suffrage, achieved in 1928, in 1930 the Women's Freedom League (WFL) joined with the National Union of Societies for Equal Citizenship (NUSEC), to deal with a major exclusion, namely that of women who married aliens. They set up The Nationality of Married Women PASS THE BILL campaign (NMWPBC) to coordinate efforts to introduce reform bills in Parliament. A key leader and campaigner was Eleanor Rathbone, who became a Liberal MP in 1930, together with a woman barrister called Crystal McMillan.

One of the key MPs to support the earlier stages of this initiative was the first woman born in England to be an MP, namely Margaret Wintringham (née Longbotham), a Liberal MP (1921 – 1924). She was also born in Keighley in 1879 and went to my grammar school, another nice touch of history. There were at least six bills during the 1930s, none of which were successful. During the Second World War, the campaign was somewhat muted, as the harsh internment of enemy aliens' policies of the British state gained precedence. By the end of the war, the incoming Labour government was more liberal and in the 1948, along with the implementation of the National Health Service and other aspects of Beveridge's 'five giant evils' the Nationality Act was passed allowing women not to be disenfranchised on marriage to an 'alien'. This 1948 Nationality Act gave such women the right to keep their nationality.

However, it turns out that it is likely that my mother was allowed to buy back her nationality, according to Clause 10 (6) of the British Nationality and Status of Aliens Act, 1914 because, although not born British, she became so aged four, when her father was naturalized in 1913, and she was a graduate and voted and had always lived in Britain, and so was deemed 'desirable' enough a person to qualify. What all of this illustrates is the ways in which aliens, émigrés, refugees, or those in exile have been treated and yet also become a fundamental part of British culture.

It has sadly taken me until now to realise how, in my very essence, I am struggling to transform gender and race policies that united my parents in their struggles. I had not given my mother the benefit of the doubt about how she had clearly influenced my desire to challenge the social and sexual structures of society. During my childhood she had been quite a conventional housewife and homemaker, only returning to work part-time as a teacher when her youngest went to secondary school. I wanted to make a different set of choices and did so, but I now wonder how hard it was for her to have to fight both patriarchy and systemic racism, in the ways in which the notion of alien or refugee were expressed at the time. Nevertheless, as second generation, as my mother was, similar to me, also meant that education became the means by which she and I struggled to transform the world in our own small ways.

Given the zeitgeist today, exacerbated by the Covid-19 pandemic, and Conservative government policies, it is very clear how there are many parallels with how migrants or refugees were treated during the Second World War. The particular harsh treatment of migrant or BAME families, especially women and children, shows how cavalier and inhumane government policies are today. Hannah Arendt, discussing Adolf Eichmann, one of Hitler's loyal deputies, at his trial in Jerusalem in 1963 used the now hackneyed phrase 'the banality of evil' (Arendt, 2006). If this is loosely translated to 'the ordinariness of inhumanity' today's zeitgeist is indeed not very dissimilar. This resonates down the generations.

Chapter 4   Here and now: how I came to be me

Alice Bondi

Here I sit in the middle of the North Pennines, a mile from the nearest house and half a mile from a road. How does the life I now lead relate to the family I grew up in, and the parents – an Austrian Jewish father and a non-Jewish British mother – who brought me up? I was born in Cambridge and lived in Surrey, from five years old. If there were any other Jews there, I was never aware of them. My family was regarded as a bit 'odd', because we ate much more adventurous food (friends coming to tea looked askance at items we considered quite ordinary), and my father had a foreign accent and wild 'mad professor' hair. I don't think I ever experienced direct antisemitism but I do wonder if the bullying I got at the grammar school (from a girl who fortunately left after our first year) had some antisemitic component to it. I certainly didn't HAVE to identify with my Jewish heritage – it wasn't something my parents pushed in any way (probably quite the opposite) and I really had little connection to anything culturally Jewish let alone religiously.

I don't know when I first was told my father's story, or any part of it. Certainly, by the time I was eight or nine, I knew enough to be aware of at least some aspects, and most probably did know about the one thing he always said he was proudest of in his life. This was not his scientific achievements, but the fact that he had sent a telegram from the UK, where he had come to Cambridge University as an exceptionally talented seventeen-year-old mathematician, to his parents in Vienna, telling them to 'leave now, without further thought'. This was March 1938, and they packed small bags (so as not to arouse suspicion) and took the train to Budapest. They crossed the border into Hungary a matter of hours before Hitler's army entered Vienna.

I later heard that Oma and Opa had made their way to the UK but after the fall of France and my father's internment in 1940, they despaired of this country and managed to get to the USA, living in New York until their deaths in 1959 and 1960. I learned of my father's internment in the Isle of Man and Canada because he told me that the island in the St Lawrence where he spent some of internment was the most beautiful place he'd lived, and because the excitement of teaching mathematics and learning about a wide range of science from fellow internees was something to which he returned and was discussed by visiting scientific colleagues who had learned their maths from him there.

I also knew he'd spent the last part of the war, after his return from Canada, doing top-secret radar research – and he told me about that because he spoke about the fun of the year he spent on the top of Snowdon, which was part of the research. His lucky escape by being on the second ship out of Liverpool rather than the first, which was without military escort and torpedoed by the Germans I learned considerably later, and quite possibly from my mother initially. She was angered by how the British government had treated Jews. I, too, was horrified to realise how Jewish refugees were regarded as suspect and suffered such privation. That definitely contributed to my fierce arguments for social justice.

My father was a committed atheist, as was my mother (brought up an Anglican) whom he met after the war. She was also a mathematician. My paternal grandparents were initially rather concerned about my father marrying a non-Jew, but once they met her (my parents went to New York to visit them) they were extremely happy that my father had a partner who entirely 'met' him intellectually. My maternal grandmother, however, made the immortal remark to my mother: 'It's not that we mind him being Jewish, dear, but he just looks so Jewish.' My grandmother was a general racist....

My parents married in 1947 and went on to have five children of which I was the first. Somehow, I became the 'memorial candle'. I was always totally fascinated by my Jewish heritage. As the oldest, I was the only one who had any memory of the Austrian grandparents we visited in New York when I was four years old (and my brother only two) – Oma lived just long enough for me to see her in hospital when we returned to the United States when I was ten, but she was barely present. We all visited my very wonderful great-aunt and the three of my father's first cousins, sisters, who lived with her in London, but my interest in drama and membership of the Junior Drama League (JDL) led me to stay with them for a few nights each Christmas and Easter holiday from when I was 11 years old, so that I could attend the JDL courses in London; hence I felt much closer to that side of my family than my siblings did. Hearing a lot of German, eating very Austrian-type cakes and being introduced to liqueur chocolates certainly contributed to my fascination!

My father was not only a scientist – he was fascinated by history and I suspect that the way he talked about it led to my own interest, and such stories as his about his grandfather gun-running for Garibaldi piqued my interest in the family's history in particular. I was the one who read the family books that arrived for my brother's non-bar-mitzvah, when I was 15, and sank into the horror of what had happened to so many of my relations. My siblings were not, and still are not, particularly interested in the complex history of the family from the expulsion from Spain in 1492, life in Genoa until 1600, in Prague before the expulsion in the mid-1740s, then in Germany before things went wrong with their business, leading to the move of my great-grandfather and his children to Vienna in the late nineteenth century.

I think all of us children were very much influenced by my parents' thoughtful, solid and active anti-racism, which connected both to my father's experience and to my mother's appalled witnessing of segregation in the southern USA when my father undertook a lecture tour when I was four years old. When he explained to me, as a child of about nine years old, what 'apartheid' was, I realised almost immediately that the power of what he told me came from the parallel with his own experience in Vienna; even though he didn't tell me much, he told me enough, combined with what a child in the early 1950s picked up, as the shadow of the war lay across everything. I think it's likely that part of my mother's reaction to segregation was informed by what she had learned from my father about what he and his family had experienced, and certainly in later life she became very keen to ensure others were aware of not only what the Nazis had done, but the way the British had treated the 'enemy aliens'. My father was always very 'understanding' of the need to intern so many, but my mother was far less forgiving.

While like any teenager I both wanted to fit in AND wanted to be defiantly different, I think my sense of identification with my foreign (and scattered across the globe) Jewish family was only partly through a wish to be different. My understanding (limited as it was) of all that had happened to my father's family gave me a very strong sense of justice: I got involved in Oxfam's Youth Against Hunger campaign; was a Labour candidate at our school's mock elections, putting a strong case for redistribution of wealth; argued with my parents about their income and what they did/didn't do with it – and more.

Ah yes, arguing. My father and I jousted frequently. He took pride in my ability to argue and really taught me through these discussions to form a good argument and use logic to make points. There was never (or very, very rarely) any unpleasantness to this – it was a case of using skill, truly listening (it's a wonderful experience for a thirteen-year-old when her father concedes a point well-made!) and expecting to be listened to.

And yet, and yet – throughout his entire life, trying to get much information about what had happened in Vienna before his departure was truly 'blood from a stone'. He claimed not to remember many things about the Judaism I knew for certain he had been well-schooled in, and referred only obliquely to the grotesque antisemitism that was in the very air he had to breathe (almost the only thing he told me was that a 'friend' became a Nazi and said 'it's not that we have anything against you personally, Hermann, but when we come to power…..'). It was infuriating trying to get the stories from him. My cousin (OK, second cousin once removed), a great family historian and I discussed swapping our efforts to get our parents' stories, since his mother seemed much more able to tell me her history of flight as a small child, and my father spoke to him more easily.

Both Oma and my mother were strong women who expected respect for their thoughts and choices, and my father did indeed respect women and talked about the inequities of women's pay etc. This probably helped me grasp feminism – which has, lifelong, been my core political and values base – more speedily and easily than some of my contemporaries. I already had gained a perception of the ways women were disadvantaged and the view that this was wrong, rather than something 'natural' as was the general viewpoint.

Only much later did I realise how Jewish, in terms of ways of thinking, much of all this was. It may not have been Torah and Talmud I was taught to dispute, but the methods of arguing were often the same. He was the most Jewish father while being fiercely anti-religion and for many years rather disdaining any identification with his Jewishness (in later life, he seemed to regain a sense of its importance to him). But in some way, I took on the importance of Jewishness, of being part of the culture and connected to the history of persecution and flight and began to find it difficult that I was not halachically Jewish.

It is probably not irrelevant to my decision to convert that I was studying psychotherapy in a context that emphasised the spiritual dimension, the importance of meaning (Viktor Frankl's *Man's Search for Meaning* had a great impact). I never ceased to be an atheist. Thank goodness no-one made me recite Maimonides' articles of belief. But so much that I learned about Judaism, Jewish culture and thought, etc, resonated with how I had come to understand the world, so it felt crucial that I could claim my Jewishness without apology for my mother's non-Jewishness. The Reform Jewish community I became a (rather semi-detached) part of led me to meet some wonderful people, including two women who have become firm friends. And I did love study sessions, teasing out meanings – I emphasised the psychological and symbolic – from passages of Torah!

My siblings don't feel like this at all, although it's interesting that they are now turning to me for the information we will need to claim Austrian citizenship. Despite a certain anxiety that my father would be turning in his non-existent grave (we scattered his ashes) to know we were going to become Austrian, he was ever the pragmatist and Brexit would have been utterly appalling to him. On that basis, he would understand our wish to take the citizenship that was removed from him, making him stateless. I think we had all grown up feeling 'European' as much as 'British' and when the vote for Brexit was passed, we were horrified. I investigated (as much on behalf of my nephew, working in the EU and wanting to continue being able to do so, as for myself) the possibility of gaining Spanish citizenship, as this had been opened up to those who could prove their ancestry back to the expulsion in 1492. This proof was relatively easily established, but in fact the other Spanish conditions (speaking Ladino, among much else!) made it quite impossible. Hence when the Austrians revised their requirements, it seemed a good route to go down, despite the worryingly right-wing tendencies still to the fore there.

I don't think it's unconnected to my background that I became a psychotherapist. It is, after all, a very Jewish profession! My own decision to go into personal psychotherapy initially (before I decided to train) was at least in part because of issues not unrelated to being second generation, and it was very strongly linked to my lifelong sense of needing to do something to create greater justice in the world. I was delighted when I first learned of 'Tikkun Olam', one of many things which cemented my sense of being Jewish.

My engagement with feminism has its roots in my father's clarity about the need to respect women's abilities, and my mother's determination to be recognised as a human being with considerable talents, and not as a 'mere woman' and most decidedly not simply as my father's wife, no matter how much renown he garnered over time. She gained a Cambridge mathematics degree and then PhD, wrote joint papers on the heat of the inside of stars with my father in the late 1940s and early 1950s and took on many rôles during her life.

I was well aware of how 'right on', socially aware, my parents were, compared to the disapproving mothers and fathers many of my friends were contending with in the radical times of the late 1960s and early 1970s. This was the era when the Civil Rights Movement, the Women's Liberation Movement, and the Gay Liberation Front were challenging accepted norms, and these ideas were all around me as a university student and on into the 1970s, as I stayed around Lancaster for a few years. Having been engaged with student protests and radical politics, feminism seemed entirely obvious when I started to read and hear about it.

My parents made all the right noises about all these things. I have to confess that when I came out as a lesbian in 1971, and wrote to tell my parents, I was secretly thinking that, if they dared make any less-than-positive comment, I would make much of having 'caught them out' as mouthing words and not following through. However, their response was swift and just right – although interestingly, it was my father and not my mother who started the letter, as was usual. I had framed my relationships with women in the context of feminism, and the 'impossibility' of equal relationships with men. My lovely father wrote: 'Infected though I am by male chauvinism, I understand what you mean. Have fun!'

It has been forgotten just how disadvantaged women were, how restricted in employment and in making our own decisions. We changed that. We developed refuges, women's centres, rape crisis phone lines. The 1970s Women's Liberation Movement had the radical idea that women were human and had the same human rights as men – and that, in the culture in which we live, women also need specific sex-based rights in order to redress the disadvantage and discrimination suffered in this society.

And we gradually convinced many people, and organisations, and even institutions. Even the Labour Party, for which I had voted, but never joined because of their lack of radical-enough politics, began to 'get it'. Laws were passed, guaranteeing women's rights and against discrimination. Stonewall was founded and pushed for the recognition of lesbians, gay men and bisexuals, and slowly things changed there (despite Margaret Thatcher's best efforts with Section 28).

The last thing in the world I was expecting was that all this, and my scientific sense of things, would be so challenged during the twenty-first century. My parents brought me up to think like a scientist, to consider facts critically, to look at possible explanations and not to assume simplistic conclusions from any presented data. They were fully aware that not everyone was well-versed in critical thinking, or in testing hypotheses, but they certainly expected me and my siblings to carry the torch for genuinely scientific thinking.

It was in my very bones that science is about testable theories, about constant change, and that good science is testable, with scientists amenable to changing their views when the evidence demands it. The notion that it represents cold, hard and immutable facts has resulted in a deluge of nonsense being put forward by the UK government (and even more, of course, by the President of the United States) during the current (at the time of writing) Covid-19 crisis. The frequently re-iterated assertion that 'we follow the science' implies that science is monolithic and simply gives 'the right answer'. As my parents' daughter, it enrages me!

I have thus always been most decidedly willing to look at new theories and to challenge accepted thinking. I had, after all, spent my adult life challenging the accepted thinking regarding the place and capability of women!

While feminism informed everything I did, including my work as a psychotherapist, I wasn't engaged in specifically feminist or lesbian campaigning in the first decade of the 21st century. But I became aware of a growing kickback against feminism, with some men asserting that 'it's all gone too far'. And, not unconnected it would seem, and insidiously, transgender ideology seeped into many parts of life. The notions that 'transwomen are women', that sex is a spectrum, that 'gender' (undefined) is innate, became truisms that could not be questioned EVEN THOUGH each of them made an appeal to 'science'.

This whole ideology is impervious to the scientific method and scientific questioning, and indeed the adherents retort 'no debate' to any attempt to analyse the theories. The mantra (that the activists specifically told us we should 'repeat after me') that 'transwomen are women' is obvious nonsense. The notion that because differences of sexual development (DSDs, also referred to as 'intersex') exist, therefore sex is a spectrum, is clearly ridiculous.

I joined the Labour Party because of my considerable concern about what was happening under the Coalition (Conservative and Liberal Democrat) government from 2010-15, with inequality and disadvantage increasing rapidly. The last thing I was expecting was that Labour would become a stronghold of gender ideology. But it did, and it gradually became clear that there were many women who felt like me and similarly found themselves under attack in our local constituency parties. Thus in 2019 I was part of the working group that established the Labour Women's Declaration, the voice of 'gender critical' women in Labour and continue to work within this group to attempt to have women's rights re-established.

Stonewall, once a major voice for LGB people, added the T and in effect became a transgender pressure group. Hence, I enthusiastically welcomed the establishment of the LGB Alliance, and undertake some voluntary work for them. In both of these campaigning groups, the sense of social justice and the importance of critical thinking and scientific analysis, approaches my parents inculcated in me, are very much to the fore. I am more and more conscious of how much I am my parents' daughter. I see increasingly clearly how my father's experience as a Jew in Vienna, and with the history he carried, informed his approach to life, to his marriage, and to bringing up children. My parents' delight in science and the creativity it brought to their lives was well-communicated to their offspring (and their grandchildren), who all continue to be active in our respective fields and lives, aware of inequalities and diversity and doing what we can to make the world better.

Chapter 5   Reflections on my life

Peter Crome

Preamble:

I am a semi-retired academic geriatrician who lives in North London. My mother (Helen Lenchen) came to the UK under the auspices of the Czechoslovakian Refugee Trust in March 1939. She was born in 1915 and grew up in Berlin but had lived in Prague since 1937. My father (Len, Lonya) was born in Tsarist Russia in 1909 and grew up in Latvia. He came to Edinburgh to study in 1927. He became a naturalized UK citizen in 1934 shortly after qualifying as a doctor.

Growing up:

In my experience, it is common for people approaching their last decades of life to reflect a little on their past, if not analytically, then conversationally with family and friends. Ancestry. com with its promise of finding you relatives you have never heard of and the consequences of Brexit are new factors that have been added to the mix alongside issues of migration, religion, politics, employment, retirement and family. I had never thought about reflecting more formally by way of an essay (I only scraped through GCE O Level English) but the request by Miriam David and Merilyn Moos has spurred me to put pen to paper. I have written about my professional career elsewhere at https://www.bgs.org.uk/bgs-presidents-biographical-sketches-peter-crome

My parents were brought up in traditional Jewish homes but they both rejected religious practice in their teens. However, my father wished to have Kaddish recited at his cremation. I had to rehearse this beforehand! My father was a highly motivated professional who took both his work, political and leisure activities seriously. My mother was a homemaker until I was able to look after myself. She then worked for the GDR trade mission in London. All of my mother's surviving family lived abroad.

I would describe my childhood as conventional but with some twists – political, geographic and historical but with the ritual aspects of Judaism touching my life only marginally. Books, music, plays and films (I was taken to the Academy and Curzon Cinemas regularly) played a large part of my early life. Zionist causes did not feature. I was taught not to believe in fairies but of course holding similar views is compatible with involvement in organized religious activities, something of which I myself am guilty.

I was born in a British hospital in Italy where my father was based after the Second World War. I was three months old when I returned to the UK. We (parents and my older brother born before the war) lived in a top floor flat in Highgate. I have only vague memories of this time and of course I do not know whether these are real memories or things that I have been told – playing in Waterlow Park, a tricycle, the 210 bus to Golders Green for shopping.

When I was four we moved to Streatham, then a courgette-free zone. We lived in a three- bed roomed detached house that was convenient for my father who had found a job as a Consultant Pathologist in Tooting. There were three other doctors who lived in the road, all of them friends of my parents – I believe that they all had undertaken postgraduate training at the same hospital. I went to Sunnyhill Road Primary School just round the corner. I played with children from my class, none of them Jewish and none with parents from abroad.

I remember playing the role of Inn Keeper in the Infants nativity play and I attended morning assembly. Somehow it must have been known at the school that I was Jewish because when we went on school journeys, I was kept back from attending the Church service that all the other children attended. I remember feeling relieved about this but did attend services, without anxiety, on a subsequent school trip to the Isle of Wight.

I do not remember being conscious of being 'other' but of course I was. I was told to tell anybody who asked about religion that I was Jewish and my family was not religious. I only had to do this once or twice and felt rather embarrassed about doing it. We did not have a mezuzah and we did not collect for Jewish or Zionist causes. We celebrated Sunday lunch (with *zakuski* and vodka) rather than Friday night dinners and my father's brother and sister and my cousins came to ours for Christmas Dinner at which Santa made an appearance. My only observances were the seder at an Aunt's house and a two-week spell at the North West London Jewish Day School when my parents were away on holiday. There I was told to copy out Hebrew letters.

The absence of grandparents was not something of which I was consciously aware. I am not aware that this absence has had any lasting effects. They lived very different lives. Only one survived the war and he lived in Israel. It was during my time at primary school that I became conscious of the continental aspects of my life. I knew where my parents came from, how they came to the UK, their political views (they were both members of the Communist Party of Great Britain), that both my grandmothers (and other relatives) were killed in the Shoah, my mother had sisters and brothers living in Israel and that her older brother had survived nine years in Nazi camps and was living in East Berlin. My parents spoke German when they did not want me to understand what they were saying. It was only later, as a teenager, that I recognized that they both spoke with a foreign accent.

At home we had visitors from all round the world and on occasions people would be 'billeted' upon us. Relatives came from Israel, au-pairs from France and we had frequent visitors from the Soviet Union as my father was very active in UK-USSR cultural relations. This internationalism meant that we had Christmas cards from all over the world, giving me a great advantage when it came to swapping postage stamps at school.

I think I must have been a bit of a show-off at primary school and I recall being called 'Cocky Crome' as I knew all the answers posed at primary school. I was no good at sport, but I enjoyed singing and country dancing classes which we had each week (often via schools radio). I used to go on my own to the museums in South Kensington and spent hours in the reference library.

At 11, I sat the examination for entry to Dulwich College and was awarded a full scholarship from London County Council. Dulwich College pretended to be an elite Public School but in reality, it was super grammar school, most of the students being on scholarships. After about 6 weeks we sat an IQ test and we were streamed into those who would do O levels in 4 years and those who would do them in 5 years. I was in the four-year stream. Further selection took place at age 13 when subjects for O levels were finalized. Having decided (or it having been decided for me) that I would go to medical school any flexibility in the choice of GCE O and A Level subjects was lost. I suppose I was a bit of a rebel at Dulwich. I decided not to join the Combined Cadet Force or the Scouts which we were expected to do as a matter of public duty!

It was at Dulwich that I first encountered any form of organized religion. This was a consequence of my parents writing Jewish on the application form. Before joining we were instructed to buy a copy of Singers Prayer Book (which I still have). I attended Jewish prayers led by teachers twice a week. I had not a clue what was going on. My first proper service I attended was a cousin's barmitzvah. I wore my school cap as we did not have any kippot at home. My father wore a flat cap and took a newspaper to read. He told me that was what his father did when he went to the synagogue. It all felt very weird. All in Hebrew except for the prayer for the Royal Family.

Adult life

I have probably written too much about my childhood but my wife, a psychiatrist, tells me that early events are important in understanding what happens in later life. So, I will whiz through my 20's to 60's more quickly before reaching the zeitgeist.

Politics

Whilst still at school I had joined the Movement for Colonial Freedom and the Anti-Apartheid Movement but played no active role. I went on a number of Aldermaston Marches sleeping on school floors and developing blisters. When I was about 15 I joined a local youth CND group which met weekly in the basement of the children's author and activist, Leila Berg. I joined the YCL but homework prevented me attending meetings. Later I joined the Communist Party Branch at King's College London where I undertook my pre-clinical studies. There were three of us, one becoming NUS President. We were later joined by a law student who became a Judge. I then moved to the Dulwich Branch of the CPGB but my involvement ended with the Soviet invasion of Czechoslovakia in 1968. I did not mind leaving the CP as I had a full social life elsewhere. I had visited Prague the year before and met František Kriegel, an old friend of my father from Spain, a member of the Czech Politburo who refused to sign the Moscow Protocol permitting the Soviet invasion.

I became active in the London Branch of the Medical Practitioners Union (now part of Unite) serving as Secretary, collecting subs etc and sitting on the MPU Council. I remain an inactive member. My first wife was a member of the Labour Party and I joined later even standing as a candidate for Southwark. Luckily I lost. One of my jobs whilst in Newcastle-under- Lyme was to sign medical chits for people who wanted postal votes. I have attended a few Labour Party meetings since returning to London in 2012.

Work

I was fortunate enough to pass both parts of the MRCP exam first time (30% pass rate) and undertook most of my postgraduate training at Guy's Hospital. Two of the three members of the appointments committee were Jewish as were both successful candidates! I first worked with Professor Harry Keen who became one of the leaders of the Save the NHS Movement. At Guy's almost all of the medical registrars undertook research for the MD degree and I did mine in the Poisons Unit. One of the perks of the job was the ability to give talks overseas and I decided to pursue an academic career, at first in London and then at Keele where I was a Professor of Geriatric Medicine and was elected President of the British Geriatrics Society. The choice of Geriatric Medicine was multi-faceted, much like the specialty itself. The combination of social, psychological and even political aspects added to complex medical conditions that many older people face made every day different and challenging. I continue to work part-time as a medico-legal expert.

I could not have achieved what success I had without the support of my wife who allowed me to spend time away when I should really have been at home. I have no doubt that I was trying to emulate my father's commitment, diligence and care and who achieved international eminence in his medical field. He only retired when he was 75. After his retirement he then wrote a book about my mother's brother, Jonny Hüttner, and his story of resistance and survival in pre-war Nazi Germany and throughout nine years of captivity in prison and three concentration camps. From a young age I had learnt about his life and his courage in opposing fascism. I have always felt that I could never live up to the example he had set. I remain in regular contact with his daughter and have visited Berlin on a number of occasions.

Judaism

Although we were secular at home my younger son told us at about the age of 6 or 7 that he wanted to have a barmitzvah. This posed a dilemma as I had not had one and there was only a miniscule, though very friendly, orthodox synagogue in Stoke. Colleagues told us about a Reform Synagogue in South Manchester. We met the Rabbi who told us that he never asked his congregants whether they were believers or not. So for the next several years we (usually me) had to take our son to the cheder every Sunday morning. I was able to do some work whilst my son did what they do a cheder and had a chance to shop at the deli. I maintained synagogue membership when we moved back to London. I am a very occasional attender at services but will go when there is an interesting evening speaker.

Family

I married, bought a house, had two children and divorced. I then downsized, married again and had a son and upsized. Both wives were secular Jews and brought new dimensions into my life. My second wife was born in Israel, grew up in South Africa, came to the UK to study, stayed, became a distinguished clinical academic and most importantly raised our son. We shared and continue to share a multitude of personal and professional experiences relevant to the zeitgeist.

My younger son, when he was 16, suddenly announced that he had to make Aliyah and move to Israel. He had just got into Oxford to study history but thankfully the Rabbi told our son that Israel needed Oxford graduates and he should delay any decision. He did but after a year as a youth worker and a Masters degree in Poland he moved to Israel, served in the IDF

Spokespersons Unit and now works for a PR firm in Tel Aviv. He has in many ways traced and followed the family history of both of sets of grandparents with their desire for a healthier, safer and farer world. His motivation has perplexed me.

Zionism and Israel

My first trip to Israel was over 40 years ago to read a paper at a conference at the Technion in Haifa. Three of my mother's siblings had gone there in 1935 from Germany as left-wing Zionist pioneers and had 'made the desert bloom'. I was taken round by my cousins and if you looked you could immediately tell the differences between Jewish villages and those for the Arab population. I kept silent. I did not return until I remarried. My wife's father and his two brothers went to Israel/Mandate Palestine having survived the Second World War in Central Asia and finding nothing left in their hometowns except the dog (Eastern Poland, now Ukraine). We continued to holiday there regularly, enjoying family hospitality and the warmth and eventually bought a holiday flat on the seaside.

The zeitgeist

So what is the zeitgeist or, Spirit of the Times, as it usually understood? I asked my children who replied Emojis, Woke, Love Island and Coronavirus. I don't think their replies were entirely serious but do confirm what I think is clear that it is unlikely that there will be a global consensus on what the zeitgeist is. Nor do I think that there would be a consensus on how one's views of the zeitgeist relate to past experiences of being the child of a German refugee.

Optimism or Pessimism?

The shadows of the Four Horsemen of the Apocalypse are around us. The traditional terrors of pestilence, war, famine and death are ever evident somewhere in the world. At times the challenges of climate change, food and water shortages seem impossible to resolve when people in least developed parts of the world have the right to a better life and those of us in the most developed world are unlikely to want to reduce their standard of living.

I am writing this at the beginning of February 2020 and I will focus on four recent events that can provide a focus for considering my personal zeitgeist and have a clear relationship to being the son of a German Jewish refugee.

Brexit: Internationalism and National Identity

I find it difficult to understand how anyone working in the NHS or higher education can support the UK leaving the European Union. The benefits of free movement have enhanced both of these sectors and, at least as far as the NHS is concerned, the whole edifice would collapse without immigrants. As an academic I have held EU grants, working and publishing with colleagues from all over Europe. One can only hope that whatever system comes into place will mirror present arrangements. I find the arguments for the isolationist "Lexit" proposition insubstantial and (the former leader of the Labour party) Corbyn's pronouncement that we must respect that result and that Article 50 had to be invoked immediately unforgivable.

Like many people in my position, I have considered taking out nationality in an EU country, as a mark of European solidarity and also to pass on to my children if they wished to live in an EU country. My elder son has married a French academic lawyer who did her PhD here. His children have both French and British nationality and he hopes to obtain French nationality too. My position is a bit more complicated for although my parents both grew up in EU countries, my claims for nationality are tenuous. My father grew up in Latvia, a country for which he had no affinity and of which he was glad to renounce citizenship when he became

British. My mother received a German pension (in respect of the years 1930-1945), some reparations and spa holidays but her nationality is not clear. I would need a lawyer to work on it. So, do I consider myself German or Latvian – no (although I love *Eisbein, sauerkraut* und *kartoffeln* and other culinary delights). I reject the definition of self through nationality. That was how I was brought up and this view has been reinforced by my life experiences. Would I seek a German passport if I was eligible – yes, if only to spite the Brexiteers!

Holocaust Memorial Day

Holocaust Memorial Day, on the day Auschwitz was liberated by the Red Army and in which my uncle Jonny was imprisoned, has become a major commemorative event in the UK. This year there were several TV programmes about the Shoah. I have spoken at a couple of events whilst I was living in Newcastle-under-Lyme, Staffordshire describing my family's experiences. Although the day is supposed to commemorate all genocides, in reality it focuses on the Shoah, perhaps understandably as this year was the seventy-fifth anniversary of Auschwitz's liberation. As with all national events, politicians use the event to promote their own agenda. In Israel it is used to support the policies of Netanyahu and his cronies. In Russia, Putin pointed out that forty percent of the victims were Soviet citizens but omits that most of these were citizens by conquest. Both of my murdered grandmothers fell into this category. I would hope that in future years the focus could be centred on other conflicts.

The Trump Peace Plan and Israel

When visiting Israel, the country of my wife's birth, where my son lives and works, and to which family members emigrated to both before and after the Second World War, it is easy for tourists to overlook the occupation of Palestinian lands, the corruption of the leadership, the uneven funding of Arab and Jewish towns within Israel, and the threat from hostile elements in Israel's neighbouring countries. As a tourist staying in an hotel, one needs to avoid the Shabbat elevator and to take account of the kosher food rules in hotels but otherwise all seems similar to a southern European city. There is a thriving economy, a vibrant cultural life and an advanced scientific sector. The failure of any meaningful peace process is depressing and the Trump plan, which legitimizes the occupation and cedes more land to Israel is clearly unacceptable to the Palestinians. The status quo with limited attacks in the Occupied Territories and short-range rockets fired from Gaza into Southern Israel is perhaps the most optimistic scenario. The chances of Israeli politicians having radically different approaches seems remote.

Burns Night Supper

This annual celebration of the life of the Scottish poet takes place on or around the anniversary of his birth in late January. My father spent his first seven years in the UK studying in Edinburgh and I like to think that makes me a little Scottish. I had to propose the toast to his memory once when I was President of the Senior Common Room! Burns was a self-made man of the Scottish Enlightenment whose liberal and humanitarian views have been an inspiration for progressives around the world. The first postage stamp to his memory was issued in the Soviet Union. Some may dispute his views of French cuisine, in this from 'Address to a Haggis':

Is there that owre his French ragout

Or olio that wad staw a sow,

Or fricassee wad make her spew

Wi' perfect sconner,

Looks down wi' sneering, scornfu' view

On sic a dinner?

On a more serious note, there is this stanza of humanity and internationalism:

> Then let us pray that come it may,
>
> As come it will for a' that,
>
> That Sense and Worth, o'er a' the earth
>
> Shall bear the gree an' a' that.
>
> For a' that, an' a' that,
>
> It's comin yet for a' that,
>
> That Man to Man the warld o'er
>
> Shall brithers be for a' that.

From 'A Man's a Man for A'That'

This message of hope has inspired the world and Burns' famous song Auld Lang Syne was sung by Members of the European Parliament just before the UK members left for the last time. Hopefully they will return soon!

Finally, and in conclusion:

I do feel at home in the UK, despite my many misgivings around the current political leadership. It has been tolerant, open and accessible. I feel privileged both materially and socially and it has given me an opportunity to thrive. Being the son of a German Jewish refugee has given me an extra positive dimension to all aspects of my life. As it turns out I would not have wished it any other way.

Further Information on Helena Crome and Leonard Crome is included in the references but also an oral account of Len's upbringing and involvement in the Spanish Civil War and the aftermath of the Second World War is available in the Imperial War Museum, London and digitally at https://www.iwm.org.uk/collections/item/object/80010949.

Obituaries:

Paul Preston: https://www.theguardian.com/news/2001/may/12/guardianobituaries1

https://www.theguardian.com/news/2001/may/12/guardianobituaries1

J. Berg, Leonard (Len) Crome - Obituary, J INTEL DIS, 45, 2001, pp. 548-548

J. Stern, Obituary - Leonard (Len) Crome, J INTEL DIS, 45, 2001, pp. 465-465

Chapter 6   Daughter of the resistance

Irena Fick

Here I am, I was born in London in May 1945 and I live in London; I could construct a C.V. making me sound as English as they come, but I was brought up between Britain and Germany and have a German accent to show for it. I am a member of the Labour Party and attend meetings to support the left, but I feel more at home in the women's liberation movement. I am in a small team producing a newsletter for the Older Feminist Network.

What made me? How did I get to be where I am? How did my individual background interact with the societies I grew up in?

I only have a hazy image of dates and the sequence of my parents' activities in the resistance, their persecution, imprisonment, and my father's trials. I know I could sit down with the documents I have collected and work on a chronological table but I'm reluctant. It would mean engaging with my family history on a cognitive and detached level. And I don't want to do that. There is a psychological barrier to get too close.

My mother: Frieda Gertrud Rosa Fick, divorced Zimmermann, née Creutzburg, 1907-1991. My father: Hans Fick, 1901-1965.

Maternal Background in the 1930s Germany:

I have found almost no documentation about my mother's resistance work. I know she was arrested several times and also kept overnight, but always released. She may have benefited from sexism: it seems conceivable that the Nazis couldn't conceive of a young woman with three children being involved in illegal political actions. Her husband was absent, doing underground work for the resistance, the Nazis were more interested in him.

In fact, my mother was in the by then illegal Communist Party and a courier in the resistance in Thuringia. Life was volatile and dangerous. One of the few things she told me about was when she was on the run with her three children (the youngest was five at the time) and had nowhere to go, she approached, close to despair, a Christian charity that operated in train stations (*Bahnhofsmission*). They provided the family with a place for the night. Normally, they would have tried to ascertain the circumstances of those requesting their services, but 'they didn't ask any questions, they must have guessed'. A small act of resistance. Forever after, every time the *Bahnhofsmission* rattled their tin, my mother would make a donation.

Arrangements were made by the Communist Party for her and the children to escape to Czechoslovakia. Her then husband was already there, but they divorced. He and their son left Prague for France under the sponsorship of the French Teachers' Union.

Paternal Background in the 1930s Germany:

I have found a number of documents from various archives about my father who was in the resistance in Düsseldorf. He was arrested in March 1933, tortured by the Gestapo, and sent to the *Esterwegen-Börgermoor* concentration camps. I know he arrived there on 9 August 1933 (pre-trial 'protective custody'). This camp was one of the earliest ones, there were fifteen camps, the *Emslandlager*, round Papenburg in North West Germany. The *Esterwegen-Börgermoor* concentration camps were relocated to Sachsenhausen by Berlin in 1936.

A few years ago, I visited the Sachsenhausen memorial site for a commemoration and was surprised that the *Peat Bog Soldiers* was performed. It was the prisoners from *Esterwegen-Börgermoor* who had built the Sachsenhausen camp. The camps around Papenburg became penal camps for convicted resistance fighters, mainly from the Rhine and Ruhr area as well as for others, such as deserters and Soviet PoWs. My father was able to escape to Czechoslovakia after his second trial for Preparation for High Treason and spells in several prisons.

Exile

My parents were both part of the refugee community in Czechoslovakia but were in danger again after the German invasion. The British government, possibly feeling uncomfortable over the Munich Agreement, agreed to take in refugees from Czechoslovakia.

In an attempt to leave, my mother was captured by the Nazis and imprisoned for three months. Eventually she was freed, perhaps as a result of her ability to present herself as harmless. 'I am divorced from my husband and my daughters are in England.' My eldest (half) sister had come to Britain via Poland, and my younger (half) sister, who was 9 at the time, on a Kindertransport from Prague.

My mother was put up by a family in Ayrshire who were already caring for my sisters and another Jewish child. But when the war started, as an 'enemy alien', my mother had to leave Ayrshire and went to London.

My father came to Britain by boat via Denmark. When internment started and tribunals classified refugees as A, B, or C, my father was originally designated C, as 'a victim of Nazi oppression'. Six months later he was reclassified B and interned in Huyton, Merseyside before being shipped off to Canada.

As far as I know, my parents moved in together in 1943. When I was born, eleven days after the liberation of Germany from fascism, they lived in Primrose Gardens, Belsize Park. When my parents moved into this flat, a woman from the Czech Trust Fund visited to offer help to set up home. When she offered them a carpet, my father, not wanting to stretch the generosity of the country that had saved his life, protested. 'We don't need a carpet.' 'Yes, you need a carpet.' came the stern answer.

My father worked in a factory, my mother made buttons at home with a little machine and the materials provided by a company. They mixed with other left-wing German and Austrian refugees, Jewish and non-Jewish, were active in the *Kulturbund*, went to the Everyman Cinema in Hampstead and to classical music concerts. They exchanged ration cards with English people, tea for sausages, I believe.

But once the war was over, Germany beckoned. My father had no desire to go back but my mother missed the language, political activity, the solidarity among the working class; she wanted to help build a new Germany. And so it came to pass that at the age of three, I was taken to Düsseldorf, in the British Zone.

We lived in a one room apartment for a while until we were granted a two-room flat, from which a Nazi was evicted. My sheltered, bubble-like childhood started.

Childhood

Düsseldorf was in ruins. My parents immediately established contact with other anti-fascists; some had survived imprisonment; others in exile in the Soviet Union. An association was formed to support survivors (VVN), and both my parents joined. My mother also re-joined the Communist Party.

On alternate Sundays my mother and my father took me along when they collected dues for the Party and the VVN, respectively. My mother took me and my friend to May Day demonstrations and rallies, ice cream as a treat. We went to VVN events, visited London where my younger half-sister, 15 years older than me, had stayed, and East Berlin where my older half-sister now lived. In case this gets confusing, I should clarify: my mother had been married and had three children with her first husband, she and my father were married in London; I am my mother's fourth and my father's only child.

When all the other little girls had a dolls pram, I got a bicycle. My father taught me how to ride it and also how to swim. My mother was in a constant state of mourning, one of her brothers had been murdered by the Storm Troopers (the perpetrators got off), another, who had been a Communist Member of the Reichstag, executed in the Soviet Union, and then there was her son. He had gone into exile with his father, but they were both captured when the Germans invaded France. My mother's first husband spent the rest of the war in a penal institution, and her son was conscripted when he was 18 and stationed in Finland. He deserted to the Soviet side but died there of typhoid. We didn't know this until later. Officially he had been reported missing. My mother listened to the *Suchdienst* (missing persons tracing service) on the radio.

By listening to the adults talk, I became aware that not all was well in Germany, it is now acknowledged that the Ministry of Foreign Affairs and the Security Services were run by old Nazis. Inge Deutschkron observed that old Nazis were even employed at the Offices for Restitution. No wonder they had an interest in harassing anti-fascists. My father needed a special diet due to his mistreatment, they costed it down to a penny to make sure he wasn't going to live a luxurious life. I have copies of the correspondence between my father, his GP, and the local Office for Restitution, making him jump through hoops.

In 1956 the Communist Party was banned after years of surveillance of its members. About 10,000 Communists continued to be persecuted in the Federal Republic of Germany, several hundred were imprisoned and had their status as resistance fighters/victims of the

Nazi regime revoked; the consequence of this was that their pension and benefits were stopped. My mother had her status and pension withdrawn but won on appeal. She suffered from this humiliation and the questioning of her integrity. The VVN provided legal support for the anti- fascists, many of the judges and prosecutors had a Nazi history.

The not so post-fascist Federal Republic also harboured ex-Nazi teachers. My parents sent me to a non-denominational elementary school, *Käthe Kollwitz Schule* – the name says it all. I had good grades. Then a decision had to be made about my further schooling. My parents asked me if I wanted to go to grammar school. I sensed reluctance, so I didn't and stayed at the elementary school. I now understand. In the GDR, then the Soviet Zone, seventy per cent of teachers were not allowed to teach because of their Nazi past, but they were welcomed in the West. Grammar schools in particular were keen to employ them, they were from the right background, could teach Latin and Greek and to hell with their morals and politics. I remember a scandal that came to light where boys in a Düsseldorf grammar school had been given an essay title 'Better Red than Dead' and an investigation showed that those who preferred being red had been given lower marks. My parents hesitated to expose me to this reactionary shabby environment.

Perhaps worth mentioning is that there were Sinti and Romani people in Düsseldorf who had survived the Porajmos but I was not aware of any Jewish presence. Both my sisters had married Jewish refugees, so in Britain and especially in the GDR, where many communist Jews had returned to, secular Jews were among our friends.

Finding my way

I spent six months in London when I was 18, working as an au pair in Golders Green. It was the time of coffee houses and the Profumo affair. I loved the non-judgemental atmosphere, went to the Hampstead Everyman and I read *The Second Sex*. I didn't get involved in anything - too shy. When I returned to Düsseldorf, I started to become involved in the peace movement but then went to live in West Berlin (following a boyfriend but also to get away from home) where, again, I was peripherally involved in the burgeoning left.

Here I also became more aware of 'ordinary Germans', people who didn't talk about fascism but about 'the war'. A neutral event. No one I met ever talked about their Nazi past, and a couple of men, who came from a resistance background didn't take me seriously. The left in West Berlin was very male orientated, women comprised the adjuncts and were marginalised. Feeling insecure and out of sorts in this environment and with no perspectives I escaped into culture. I was working with dodgy people for a company involved in dodgy deals, going on demonstrations and visiting my sister in East Berlin, partaking in the vibrant theatre culture there. After about 18 months I decided I had had enough. Hey, I was British born, I had a British passport.

I arrived with my British passport at the same time that Kenyan Asians came here, I remember the fuss and thinking they are more British than I am and no one questioned me. I found a job in a trade union, joined the Communist Party, and lived in Belsize Park, where else? Then came the women's liberation movement and a new phase of life started. This was new, this was different from the women's emancipation my parents and their friends supported. This applied to me. In West Berlin I had started reading Frantz Fanon's *The Wretched of the Earth* until I came to the passage where the fighters leave the village and the women stand on the side and cheer them on. And I had thought I was part of it, there I was on the sidelines. I was devastated, I stopped reading (I never finished the book).

Women's liberation made sense.

For all my life in Britain (I did move away from Belsize Park, studied and worked as a teacher, trade union official, freelance translator and interpreter) I adapted, tried to fit in, acquired a couple of social skills, made friends, etc. Germany didn't leave me. I still feel that anger, and hurt, about what happened and happens there and how so many people deny the past and detach themselves from it. The picture younger Germans form about the Holocaust comes from lessons in school, so they know – something. Then there is another layer, films, both dramas and documentaries, and the carefully choreographed films of Nazi rallies and Nazi Party Congresses we can't help being familiar with as they are repeated, taken out of the cupboard for anniversaries. The stock images of Jews being forced onto lorries. The six million.

Actually, as Helen Epstein points out, it was between 11 and 13 million. Jews are the largest group, about half of all the people murdered. In Germany the six million are commemorated, others are rarely mentioned. The three and a half million Soviet Prisoners of War, gay men, disabled people, Jehovah's Witnesses, Freemasons, communists, social democrats and other opponents of the Nazis, among them Christians; Polish intellectuals, Soviet Commissars, so called *Asoziale*, among them homeless people and many young people who just didn't fit in, and Sinti and Roma people. Black people and Chinese Germans and Chinese nationals suffered. Then there are the victims in the countries occupied by Germany and enslaved labourers. Yet both here and in Germany we know about Auschwitz. Auschwitz, the metaphor for the whole well-organised, industrially operated annihilation machine. The history of fascism in Germany is more nuanced.

German young people know about the Holocaust, but do they ask their grandparents where they stood and what they did? Their grandparents have always been nice to them, no way could they have been Nazis! When I come across young Germans, I always give them a light grilling. I don't really mind if their grandfather was a mass murderer, what I am interested in is how they respond, whether or not they are interested and engaged, whether or not they have asked their nice grandfather or great-grandfather what their involvement was. Reactions are mixed, some understand what I'm after, others are irritated – and show it. They'd rather not know.

But the same can be said about Britain in relation to its imperialist past. There is the same divide, the history of colonialism a fact, yet only rarely do we hear about atrocities, and there were plenty. I always ask white people who were born in India, for example, what their parents did there, and the answer is always non-committal. They'd rather not know. Also, Britain is the only country which has not had war crimes trials. In the Channel Islands Nazi collaborators carried on doing their jobs unmolested. There is a rift between the cognitive, the cultural, and the emotional, the family lore, between knowledge and understanding.

And how do we, children of resistance fighters, process these different levels. Objectively, my parents were heroes but I'm not putting them on a pedestal. They were caught up in a system that they had fought to prevent. They were modern parents, but they also prevented me from doing things I wanted to do – they were probably right but it didn't feel like that at the time. I rebelled just as much as other children and teenagers. I acknowledged but thought little about how deeply I was formed by my parents and the society I was brought up in. I lived, had several careers, each lasting about a decade, was involved in trade union disputes, had several serious relationships, each lasting about a decade, had a child, lived life.

It was only in my fifties, when I heard of the Second-Generation Network that I decided to take part and think about how my parents' past had influenced me. In the last twenty or so years I have thought a lot about my history and what it means. I also question my attitude. When people ask me about my accent, I tell them I am German, but add that I was born here and that my parents were refugees or, depending on who it is that wants to know, that they were in the resistance. I could kick myself for it, what does it have to do with them? I do it to distinguish myself from what I call 'Nazi Germans'. Why do I feel this is necessary? I don't have to justify my existence.

As part of acknowledging my specific history, i.e. non-Jewish refugee background, the Second-Generation Network didn't quite do it for me, but it took me some years to pluck up courage to visit the *Memorial Emslandlager*, and I wouldn't have gone on my own. I wanted to go and see and face the place, at the same time I dreaded it. I dreaded the emotions the place might evoke. My son agreed to come along to hold my hand, and I found that my hesitation was unnecessary. The people who run the place knew exactly how to deal with me, they knew how to keep the emotions down while at the same time acknowledging my connection with the history of the site. I wasn't the first and I won't be last to face the place where our fathers faced hell.

I have been to two conferences for the Second Generation in Papenburg, arranged by the Memorial Emslandlager and am now in contact with the Children of the Resistance North-Rhine Westphalia (*Kinder des Widerstands NRW*) and work with them as much as is possible from London.

Chapter 7   Thoughts on being a second-generation Jewish refugee

Sybil Gilbert

A Brief Background

My mother was a refugee from Germany. She fled to England after being accepted on the sponsored domestic scheme. She had previously applied to train as a nurse, but complications over exit visas meant that she lost that opportunity. She lived in Breslau, now Wraclaw in Poland. My grandfather had been taken to Buchenwald on *Kristalnacht* but released. Her parents had fled to Roermond in Holland as no organisation in any other country would offer my grandfather work even though he was a professor of engineering. My grandparents were deported when Holland was occupied and were taken from Westerbork to Terezin and, finally, Auschwitz where they were killed. My father was English but hid his Jewishness during captivity post Dunkirk. He was taken with his fellow prisoners on a 'death march' before liberation. He submitted written evidence for the Nuremberg trials.

After arriving in the United Kingdom in March 1939, my mother narrowly escaped internment after a grilling by the Liverpool police (she was a domestic in a Birkenhead household). The grilling left her distraught and seemed to turn on confusion over spelling her name with the German double 's'. The family she was with treated her like a slave; the lady of the house was especially cruel. She had a second unhappy experience as a domestic in the South West of England. During the rest of the war, she ended up as a telephonist for the Fire Service. I fail to understand how, with her strong accent, she got this post when she had been turned down twice by the Land Army because she was a non-British alien. Interestingly, I only found out about these two rejections when looking through her papers after her death. I guess she had found yet another rejection so painful that she erased it from her oral history. Her elder brother was interned in Canada after a brief internment in the Isle of Man (he died when I was a toddler so I have no recollection of him). Her younger brother (who had come over with Kindertransport) was sponsored by an 'adopter' and went to a public boarding school.

My Childhood and Career

I grew up in Birmingham. There was an informally linked *Mittel European* Jewish community. Living in our road alone was our GP (a Polish Jewish refugee) and, also, the head of Birmingham blood transfusion service (a Czech Jewish refugee). Many of these refugees (including my own family) were totally secular and the Birmingham Chamber Music Society provided a home from home where they bonded over Beethoven and Schubert quartets. I was totally and innocently unaware that my cultural background was in any way 'different' from that of a typical English family until I left home for university.

None of my friends in Birmingham (most of them non-Jews) were religious, my secondary school had quite a few Jewish students and, until I went to university in London, I had never encountered antisemitism. Ironically, as a small child, I did get upset when on a couple of occasions, my mother was verbally abused because (shortly after the war) people realised from her accent that she was German. When I did encounter antisemitic comments at university, I was deeply upset and angry; especially so as these comments were being made by intelligent and well-educated people. My reaction was to join the university 'Jewish Society' and go to a Liberal Schul with one of my paternal aunts. Antisemitism made me feel more, not less, 'Jewish' and I resented my parents for not giving me the opportunity to be part of Yiddishkeit. I felt that I had been deprived of my heritage. I realise with hindsight that they both wanted desperately to protect me from prejudice and worse and had wanted me to become a middle-class English woman with no traumatic back story. However, the experience has led me to perhaps understand why members of minority groups band together in the face of criticism of one of their members (whether that criticism is justified or not). I feel that this might explain the reluctance of many Muslims to openly condemn extreme fundamentalist preaching even though they do not themselves hold those views. The immediate instinctive reaction to attack, verbal or otherwise, is to protect your 'tribe'.

I became an academic lawyer. I had been hopeless at and disinterested in science at school to my father's despair as he wanted me to be a doctor; a career denied to him by his poverty. He had grown up in the Commercial Road in East London, the son of East European Shtetl Jews. However, when I said that I wished to read law, he was mollified (the old doctor or lawyer stereotype). I married a non-Jewish lawyer, but we were then working in London and within our professions had many Jewish friends, so I felt no sense of isolation. Being a non-religious Jewish second-generation refugee was not so unusual among largely secular Jewish colleagues.

The Impact on My Life

My mother had become seriously ill when I was at university and died when I was in my early twenties. We had been emotionally, very close. It was more than the fact that I was an only child. My mother's health had precluded her from having more children. The closeness was the direct impact of what had happened to her and to her family. Almost all of her maternal family had been killed. Of those who survived the war, her elder brother had died at a cruelly young age of kidney failure. Her younger brother (to whom she had been a substitute mother as he had come to England via Kindertransport at the age of eight) emigrated to Australia in the early 1960s. She clung to me as her raison d'etre (a heavy burden for any child, but one

I believe many of us second generationers have born). She was wildly over-protective and suspicious of any boyfriend relationship that might possibly lead to marriage. None the less, we shared a love of literature, classical music and spent many hours going around art galleries together.

She gave me my love of European culture. I do not think that my mother ever recovered psychologically from her experiences. She had had an idyllic childhood in Germany before the Nazis gained power. She referred to Germany as 'home'. She spent many hours showing me photographs of her family and talked about growing up in a cosmopolitan environment where travel within Europe and marriages between those living in different European countries was the norm. Despite everything, she said that the Holocaust could have happened anywhere. She spoke German on her deathbed. She was definitely an exile. I remember seeing a TV documentary about Howard Jacobsen returning to ancestral roots in Germany and stating that 'unrequited love is the hardest to bear'. A country that had granted freedoms to Jews and had endorsed widespread assimilation had then rejected them in a spectacular way. My mother definitely suffered unrequited love for her place of birth.

My parents were married until my mother's death in 1974 and my father never remarried keeping everything in the house untouched as a memorial to her. My father had much more hatred for Germany than my mother. He was the reason that I was not brought up bilingual--another source of niggling resentment, but I guess the world was a different place in 1948 when I was born. The diktat 'no word of German will be spoken in this house' was not observed on the many occasions that my parents wished to have a conversation without me being able to understand them. My father spoke fluent German. His parents were Yiddish speakers and he had studied languages at university. So, I was a dispossessed Jew and a dispossessed German. What my father did give to me was rigid sense of morality (almost Kantian). We would spend much time debating issues at the dinner table. I guess morality and politics (not in the party political sense, but in terms of the social contract) took the place of Torah discussion in our household.

My career as a law lecturer came out of my interest in law as a remedy for injustice. I have an almost visceral response to injustice of any kind. My specialist subject areas covered due process rights, human rights and constitutional protections. Whether I would have turned to this field in any event, I do not know. I am sure that the idea came from my study of constitutional history at school. I was a very reserved child but lost all fear when arguing the case for someone I felt had been wronged. My politics is linked to my professional life. Social justice is an important issue for me. So is internationalism and the absence of racism. How far my background fostered this, I cannot say.

What I do know is that my parents spent many hours of my childhood pouring through documents and filling out forms for compensation from the German government, which activities rarely produced any result. So, the fight for justice was observed by me as a small pre-school child even though I did not understand what was going on. You would scarcely consider it a normal family weekend to spend it in the empty office of a friendly solicitor, taking advantage of his permission to use the ancient precursor of the Xerox machine. I have to say that my father was also a fighter for the oppressed (in his eyes my mother) and had battled the Home Office and his MP on her behalf. His father (my paternal grandfather) had been a semi-Bolshevik agitator for workers' rights in his sweat shop, so I cannot put my political attitudes and career entirely down to the fact that my mother was a refugee.

How far has this influenced my personal life? I was married for over forty years until the death of my first husband. I am now happily remarried. Neither of my husbands was/ is Jewish. As a secular Jew, I have nothing in common with an Orthodox lifestyle. My first husband was a lawyer and mixed with so many Jews that he was effectively counted as one. He was quite happy for this to be the case. He practised as a barrister in the first multi-racial set of chambers in the Temple. He was totally at home with Jews, Muslins and Hindus and West Indians, all of whom we socialised with and shared meals with. I later realised that I had been living in an unusual (for that time, at least) international bubble.

In 2000, I moved to live in the Isle of Man. I had not intended to become permanently resident there, but circumstances due to my first husband's ill health effectively trapped me there. I joined the local Hebrew community (very small and in no way orthodox) but was always unable to feel part of the wider community because of the Christian centred culture that relentlessly pervades the island. I am sure that there is no deliberate intention to make non-Christians feel 'othered'. People there are apparently kind. Rather it is the inability of an insular community to appreciate that there are those who do not wish to go to a church service on 'Civic Sunday' or take part in 'processions of the cross' at Easter and that this does not make them strange or anti-social people.

Anyway, my second husband (originally from Wembley) and I moved back to the Warwick/ Leamington Spa conurbation last summer and I feel a sense of liberation. I now live in a cosmopolitan, culture rich environment with two universities within twelve or so miles of my house and Birmingham and central London are accessible by train. I guess that, for me, a largely rural, mono-cultural Christian society just feels very oppressive and I needed to pack my bags and move on even though I am not a synagogue attender. I do not ascribe this feeling solely to my mother being a refugee; however, I have always been ready to 'move on' to another job or another town without feeling tied by family connections.

So, I consider myself Jewish even though I am not religious and I wonder if perhaps I may not have done so had it not been for the suffering of my family and that of Jews as a whole. Does thousands of years of oppression reinforce an identity? I think it does. However, that said, ultra-orthodox religious Jews make me feel, as a fellow Jew, uncomfortable. Partly, this is because I have an aversion to the precept of living according to unquestioning faith and to the reading of religious texts without historical context or rational analysis. It matters not whether the religion is Christianity, Islam or Judaism. I am fundamentalist averse. Partly, my discomfort is because the Hassids of North Manchester and Stamford Hill make me aware that their outward 'otherness' invites notice and hence antisemitism.

This is, I think, a direct effect of my second-generation refugee status. I suspect that, along with many others in my situation, I was brought up to 'blend in'. As a small child, I was always aware that I must not draw attention to myself in public. My mother insisted that any bad behaviour took place at home. Outside of the home, I must behave impeccably. I still catch myself being almost obsequiously polite on occasion when speaking to shop assistants, hairdressers, doctors' receptionists and others. Only when something cannot be resolved other than by my asserting myself, does my fighting persona reluctantly emerge--that is unless, strangely, I am fighting the system on behalf of someone else when I go in all guns blazing!

I am a Zionist in that, although I hate what Netanyahu has done to Israel and I think that aggression breeds aggression, I believe fervently that the state has a right to exist. I also believe in the 'no more lamb to the slaughter' ethos and am proud that I was born in the year that Israel was formally recognised as a country. If I had been born in other circumstances as some-one else, who knows, I might have been waving an extreme left-wing flag for BDS. Instead, I just feel sad that a country that we saw as one positive hope after the Holocaust (my cousin fought in the 1967 war and his children were in the IDF) has behaved in ways that can be criticised. None the less, I still love all the good things that Israel stands for.

I resent the word Zionism being used as a term of abuse and as implying that anyone who supports the existence of Israel also supports extreme 'Trumpian' politics. There are lots of good things going on in that country and it is true (whilst not waving a flag for Likud or the extreme right-wing parties that support Likud) that Israel is expected to behave according to a higher moral standard than other countries. This is not to say that Israel does not deserve criticism when justified and though peace and integration initiatives happen at ground level, we need modern day prophets such as Amos Oz to raise the level of the public debate. In its creation post-1948, Israel has never experienced real peace and two generations of Israelis and Palestinians have been fed memes of anger and hatred.

As for reconciliation, I am taking my own personal peace initiative by claiming restored German citizenship. I think that populism is a real threat to Western democracy. Germany, alone, has experience of where this can lead. Small steps to the gas chamber. We have not yet learnt the dangers of treating groups as 'the other'. Germany may have done so, or at least is more sensitive to the risk of escalation from what appears to be fringe politics--at least at present! The combined factors of Brexit, my love of European culture and my admiration for Angela Merkel have impelled me to take this step. I have no idea whether I will succeed as I come under the new discretionary leniency being extended to those born legitimately who do not technically fall under Article 116 as their father was not German and they were born before 1953. Whatever the outcome, it has meant a rereading of documents and personal letters dating back to 1938.

I have mentally rerun the traumas of my mother and it has, inevitably, upset me, not least because I feel anger that the family left it too late and trusted (as many others did) that the situation could not get worse. Daniel Finkelstein has expressed it concisely in saying that the optimists did not survive. The pessimists fared better. I have (not through personal choice) no children and so the family story will not survive through them, but I have donated some papers to the Weiner Institute Library and the children of my maternal cousins in Australia have now shown an interest in the Gross-Sachs saga. I guess the effects of being a second generationer are that I have suffered the deprivation of maternal family members and have often found myself unintentionally 'othered' even by well-meaning people. Perhaps because I do not belong to a schul, I find it harder to have a cultural identity, but I think that, as a consequence, I am a reasonably independent, tolerant and outward looking person. I always cope with life's many setbacks and difficulties, by reminding myself that compared to deportation to a concentration camp, the situation is hardly serious!

I write this last paragraph in April 2020 as a kind of post-script. I have been asked to reflect on the impact of Covid 19 on my second-generation status. I wrote in an earlier paragraph about my joy of once more living in an area where academic and cultural activities abound and where visits to London and other cities are once again feasible. All of these benefits are for now (and at least for the foreseeable future) off the agenda. I am 71 years of age and, if the experts are correct, it will be at least a couple of years before a vaccine is widely available. This will, inevitably rule out concerts, art exhibitions, train travel and air travel unless appropriate masks are worn and social distancing is observed. However, many people world-wide will also be feeling the same deep sense of loss. The joyful internationalism of the classical music world will, sadly, be drastically curtailed for a long time to come.

On a deeper level, the sharing of cultures and ideas is not just an ideal, it is part of my identity (inevitable with my mixed Russian, Polish, French and German Jewish heritage). I am saddened that the drawbridges between countries, have been pulled up, albeit perhaps necessarily at present. Asylum seekers and those fleeing war are likely to be repulsed even more strenuously than before and this protectionism may endure way past the Covid threat. I cannot say that my sadness is influenced specifically by my mother's experience, but it must have some part to play. However, being without family (I have cousins, but apart from two, they are spread around the globe; Israel, America, Australia) I am more accustomed than the many who have a traditional British family life to communicating virtually. As someone who was deprived from birth of close family members living within a local community, or even within the same country, I do not feel the acute sense of deprivation that others might in the current situation. The aspect of this pandemic which I *do* think impacts more deeply on me is 'lock down'. There is a real feeling of imprisonment. The need to be ready to flee, to be able to 'up sticks' without restraint is deeply embedded in my psyche. I know that this feeling is irrational. The mantra circulating on social media that I should think of my home as a safe place and not as a prison does not sit well with me. There is a gut feeling of panic that I cannot go where I want to or reside wherever I wish, and material comfort is irrelevant.

Chapter 8   Questioning Jewish Identity

Maggie Gravelle

Introduction

By the summer of 1944 my parents, both Jewish refugees, were sufficiently confident about the outcome of the war to start a family and I was born in spring 1945. We lived in Sheffield where, two years later, my brother was born. In 1952 we moved to a suburb of London and I went to a girls' grammar school. It had always been assumed that university would be the next step and I got a place at the University of Leeds to study Sociology. When, after a year of post- graduate study, I left university I was committed to working on the Educational Priority Area research and in preparation joined the ILEA Research and Statistics Department. It was during this time that I decided to 'return to the chalk-face' rather than pursue an academic career and spent the following years teaching in inner city schools, eventually specialising in teaching children from multilingual backgrounds. My final post was in a university teacher education department.

The main motivation for my choice of career and of working in inner city institutions has been my commitment to establishing equality in diversity. From contact in my first school with children from disadvantaged backgrounds to my final post in a university department with students from a variety of ethnic origins, I have been aware of the discrimination they face, from individuals and institutions. Some of these values can be traced to the atmosphere of tolerance and lack of prejudice that pervaded my childhood.

My parents' values

In 2010 both my parents died. They were in their nineties and I think they would have added, 'at the end of a long and happy life'. Certainly, they were both refugees from Hitler and had experienced the prejudice, cruelty and injustice meted out to Jews in Germany and Austria, but they met and married after arrival in England and remained devoted to each other for the next sixty-five years. With their deaths, I became more aware of the gaps in my knowledge of our family history and took time to learn more. I also came across documents I had not known about and photographs of people I could not place.

My parents were naturalised in 1947 and thought of themselves as British. Both of them clearly articulated their appreciation of the freedom and liberalism of British life and of the refuge it gave them. They were not exiles having no intention of going back, nor did they see themselves as aliens. I have a copy of a Security report on my father from when he landed at Croydon airport in 1938. He received this in 2002 and it refers to him as 'the alien', a term which he would have rejected. Much later he wrote:

> We were called 'enemy aliens' and tribunals were set up to interview us to ascertain whether we were likely to be hostile or whether we were genuine refugees who had no loyalty to Germany. In fact, most of us would have done anything to help the allies. (private paper)

In 1940 he was briefly interned at Prees Heath as an enemy alien but did not appear to resent the experience and later described it as quite stimulating due to the number of interesting and knowledgeable people he met through what was described as the Prees Heath University. In an interview my father gave in 2004 he ends with the following words:

> We are British patriots and love the country and the people. In the nearly fifty years since I have lived here, my religion, race, former nationality, etc. have never come to

be issues and I have never been disparaged by friends or authorities. That is why I do not feel like a person living in exile, and I am happy that I can live my life without prejudice from the authorities and fellow citizens, based only on performance and contribution, free and unhindered.

My mother, Annemarie, similarly, saw herself first and foremost as British. Although she took Austrian citizenship on marriage so that should this be necessary, she and my father could remain together, she did it with a heavy heart. She felt at home and accepted in England. Like my father, she was without personal prejudice and readily made friends with people from all backgrounds. They greatly valued the liberalism that they experienced in the UK at the time and instilled in me and my brother a strong sense of social responsibility.

My parents' background

Kurt was born in Vienna in 1916, the second son of a well-established, middle class Viennese family on his mother's side and of a family originating in Bohemia on his father's. They lived in Leopoldstadt, a Jewish quarter in central Vienna. Certain Jewish festivals were celebrated as a matter of tradition rather than of faith. Home life was comfortable and in general his memories of his early life were warm and filled with love and friendship and many outdoor activities, although tinged with an awareness, even then, of antisemitism.

Family values were very strong and, in my father's case, centred around his maternal grandmother who made what he considered unreasonable demands. He remembered with some bitterness the weekly visits to his grandmother and how they affected his own freedom. He and his brother had to visit her every week and to sit in silence unless spoken to. If they misbehaved, they had to kneel before her and ask forgiveness. Perhaps he resented the power she exerted over his mother and the possible impact that this had on his father's position in the family.

Kurt was an able but lazy student and always something of a rebel. In 1934, when he entered the university, life in Vienna was becoming increasingly difficult for Jews and he became active in the underground Student Socialist movement. Early one morning in 1937 he was arrested and spent three weeks in prison under interrogation but was eventually released without charge. Later that year, restrictions were tightened and he could no longer attend university.

By 1938 and the *Anschluss* it became clear that he would have to leave Austria. He managed to get sponsorship from an English couple whom he had met on a skiing holiday and also bribed an official to obtain an exit visa. Before he could leave, however, he was rounded up together with hundreds of other Jews and incarcerated in a school. Despite this he managed after a few days to get an interview with a Gestapo officer whom he convinced that he had a visa and was due to leave Austria anyway. He was released on condition that he left the country within twenty-one days. His brother and father also managed to leave, but his mother, grandmother and great aunt were murdered in Auschwitz.

My paternal grandfather lived with or near us for the remainder of his life. He was a confused and lonely man who never settled properly and whose English remained poor. I suspect he felt guilty that he had survived while his wife and family had not. He was rarely cheerful and gave the impression that life had defeated him. But I remember him as very affectionate. My father, on the other hand, was resentful of the hold that his maternal grandmother had over the family and probably held her partly responsible for the death of his mother.

As a child I was unaware of the details of Kurt's life which were never discussed at home. Looking back, I think that this had the effect of involving him to a greater extent than was conventional in his immediate family. So, we had a father who shared some of the tasks of child-rearing and domesticity. I have a memory of being pushed in a pram by him. During my early childhood, in Sheffield, my parents were close friends with a British young family. The adults were socialists and trade unionists for whom education and opposition to injustice were paramount. They remained friends for life.

My mother, Annemarie, was born in 1919 to a wealthy German family, the Meyers. Both sides of the family were merchants and bankers – traditional Jewish occupations. Her father was in some ways a conventional 'pater familias' expecting respect and home comforts. He saw his role as providing for the safety and well-being of the family, but he was also independent-minded and prescient.

My mother appears to have had quite a lonely early childhood. She and her older sister were looked after by a series of *kinderfräulein*, but since there was an eight-year age gap, Annemarie was often on her own. The main contact with her parents was rather formal, although she remembered with some nostalgia a time when she was ill in bed and her mother spent many hours reading to her. At the age of six she went to school. Here she was happier, made friends and enjoyed the lessons.

Although, before the war, the Meyers had celebrated the main Jewish festivals they were not religious and did not attend synagogue. My mother remembered the role she had to play as the youngest member of the family at the Seder meal but said she was not really aware of being Jewish until she went to secondary school where one of the subjects was Religious Education. Jewish children were taught separately for these lessons and it was here that she learnt to read, without understanding, basic Hebrew. Her father, who was fiercely anti- religious and vigorously opposed to Zionism, was incensed at this practice but did not go so far as to withdraw her from lessons. Several years later, when the family settled in England, he deliberately chose an area of London which was not predominantly Jewish in which to live.

By 1933, when Hitler came to power, it was impossible to ignore one's Jewish heritage. My mother remembered the Brown Shirt bullies in the streets and the fact that many of her classmates and erst-while friends joined the Hitler Youth. School became very uncomfortable, particularly after she refused to *Zieg Heil*. The Jewish Boycott galvanised the family into action and Annemarie was sent to boarding school in Switzerland, only coming back to Berlin in holiday times. In 1936 the family left Germany permanently, moving some of their money and a surprising quantity of goods, including some large pieces of furniture, to England.

The Meyer family was a slightly distant, formal part of my life from early days. Their house was large and slightly intimidating – we were always on 'best behaviour'. When we lived in Sheffield we travelled to London for Christmas and later when we moved south for my father's job, saw my grandparents, aunt, uncle and cousins more frequently, but mainly on special occasions such as my grandmother's birthday, (I do not remember any celebrations of my grandfather's birthday), Easter and Christmas. These Christian festivals were absorbed into the household rituals with Easter eggs and Christmas trees and presents, although devoid of any religious content. So, I never had any religious up-bringing from either side of the family and any sense of Jewish heritage was tempered by a strong desire to integrate into British society.

Personal identity

So, I am a second-generation Jew, but this has never been a significant part of how I define myself. There are four strands that I think are particularly influenced by my parents and their experiences; feminism, equality particularly anti-racism, and multilingualism. The fourth strand is Jewishness and religion.

Feminism

First and foremost, I would describe myself as a woman and a feminist, although I have never joined a women's group. Rather, I see feminism as a lens though which to understand, relate to and evaluate institutions and individual behaviours.

From my grandparents and accounts of my great grandmother I had a model of womanhood that centred around their husbands, the home and the children. Men went out into the world to develop careers, provide for their families and to engage with the 'big' political and economic decisions of the day, whereas women's sphere of influence, in which men were fairly passive, was the home. My Meyer grandfather was surprised, and slightly shocked, at the level of involvement that Kurt had with his young family. He also found his grandchildren rather too undisciplined I suspect.

From my mother, of course, I had a somewhat different perspective. She was, in some ways, an unusually 'liberated' woman. She had a good education and from the time she went to boarding school had been fairly independent. She had studied physics, a very 'male' subject, at university, first in London when she could live at home, but later in Bristol where she lived in some rather chaotic digs full of friendly and uninhibited people of all backgrounds. It was in Bristol that she met my father. She had a number of relationships before she married and her views on sex and marriage were refreshingly modern. Evidently, my grandfather was somewhat relieved that she managed to find a suitable husband since she was 'damaged goods'.

Even after her marriage she went out to work first as a technician in a research lab and later as a translator. Although she stopped work when we children arrived, she returned as soon as we went to school, finding child-rearing a rather tedious interlude. She had an abortion later when she and my father decided that they wanted no more children and her brief stay in hospital was explained to my brother and me as 'having her insides cleaned out', a description that I accepted without question.

My mother and I had many conversations about feminism and women's roles and she was supportive, and slightly envious, of my continuing to work part-time while my children were still young. But we disagreed about the nature of the inequality between men and women. She took the view that men and women, although nominally equal, were fundamentally different, not only biologically but also emotionally, and therefore some roles were more suited to the male and others to the female temperament. She saw this as natural rather than socially determined. This despite the recognition that the roles that women took because they were 'better at them', were generally regarded as inferior to those of men. I found this rather shocking from a woman whom I had thought of as equal to my father and who had carried on with a career after marriage and children.

In considering a career, I was not consciously influenced by feminism, but it was through being a teacher that I became increasingly aware of gender inequalities and low expectations, which I had not experienced to the same extent in my own up-bringing. The first piece of research that I did (1982) while working in a girls' school, was to investigate the extent to which girls interpreted apparently neutral language through gendered eyes. I became very aware of the images and accounts of both women and black people in educational and children's literature and beyond.

Equality and anti-racism

My feminism is closely linked to a commitment to equality, the foundations of which were laid at home. It is impossible to ascertain the extent to which parental influence shapes one's views and decisions, but in my case, it seems to form the bedrock for later experiences. That respect and consideration were afforded to everyone was an underlying value and principle, largely as a result of my parents' experiences. This was evident in the way in which they treated people in personal, social and work situations.

In London we lived in a middle-class suburb where the majority of inhabitants were white, middle class British people. There was a flat on the top floor of our house which, at one stage, was let to nurses from the local hospital. One of these was an east African, Mr. Adedayo. He was a charming man who used to enjoy walking round our garden with Annemarie while she pointed out all the different flowers and vegetables. He was the first black person I had been in close contact with and his colour was never an issue.

During the 1956 Hungarian Revolution my parents offered a home to the son of a refugee family. As far as we children were concerned this chiefly meant a change to our sleeping arrangements since the boy would share a bedroom with my brother and I would move into a small bedroom of my own. There were a number of meetings with the boy's aunt and final arrangements were well underway when she mentioned the fact that the family would assume her nephew would continue with a Catholic education. This was impossible to contemplate and so the arrangement fell through.

The offer had been made in order to give sanctuary to a child who was suffering, as they had in the past. It was an example to me of their commitment to equality and personal liberty and of their integrity in ultimately feeling unable to compromise their principles.

In my case this commitment to equality, and in particular to anti-racism, has developed throughout my life. As a teacher I generally chose to work in schools in working class, multiracial areas. When my own children were small I took a Home Tutor post, working with a very diverse range of pupils. One was from a single parent (father) family who would otherwise have been in an children's home. His main skill was breaking into cars and even as a twelve-year old was a confident driver. Another boy was a school-refuser. He rebelled against teachers who discriminated against him on the grounds of his colour, on one occasion abandoning him at a distant school playing field because he did not have the right kit. A young, pregnant girl was not allowed to go to school because she was deemed to set a bad example for other pupils. She and her parents lived in an immaculate, but tiny pre-fab. in which the baby was going to grow up.

Later, as a secondary teacher in the East End, I worked closely with Bangladeshi pupils, some of the most disadvantaged in the area. It was here and through a secondment to the Centre for Urban Education Studies, that I developed a greater understanding of racism. I joined the editorial team of *Issues in Race and Education*, a journal devoted to exploring racism and ways of combating it through education. I became a member of the Anti-Nazi League and an enthusiastic protester and I read widely about issues connected with race and racism, including submitting evidence to the Swann Inquiry, *Education for All* (1985). In 1986 I went with a group of teachers from Tower Hamlets on a study tour of Bangladesh. This was intended to give us a greater insight into the backgrounds of our pupils, which it certainly achieved, but it also hardened the resolve to provide a fairer environment for those growing up in the UK.

The Macpherson Report (1999) into the killing of Stephen Lawrence led me to a greater understanding of the insidious nature of racism and particularly of 'institutional' racism. A commitment to anti-racism continues to this day through my volunteering role with a local refugee charity. Much of the hatred and intolerance directed at refugees is connected to personal prejudice but the institutional racism is more difficult both to detect and to remedy.

Multilingualism

German language was part of my early childhood, although when I began to respond in English my parents readily gave up this link to their past. I regretted this later when I placed greater value on languages and spent one holiday with a German family trying to improve my spoken German. But it also imbued in me a discomfort with many aspects of German and Germany. Consequently, as an adult I have rarely travelled to Germany or Austria and, though strongly pro-European, did not seriously consider taking out German nationality following Brexit.

From when I started school mostly English was spoken at home, although with my grandparents conversation was often in German – the language they were most comfortable with. I still retain some understanding of German, although my vocabulary remains child-like and I was always aware that in comparison with my parents and grandparents my German was halting and my pronunciation poor and was therefore embarrassed to use it.

My mother's parents had brought some of their possessions out of Germany and these included some children's books. I remember looking through *Struwelpeter*, which seemed very harsh and spiteful, and another German book, *Etwas von den Wurzelkindern*, which was beautifully illustrated and involved children who lived in the roots of a tree. I also remember being read to from a German version of The Pied Piper of Hamelin and enjoyed joining in with parts of the story – *'So viel Gelt hab Ich nicht.'* On the other hand, my parents were not familiar with the traditional English nursery rhymes and stories, which I suppose my brother and I picked up from school. As a child I loved fairy stories, reading all the Andrew Lang series which I borrowed from the library.

Although I would not claim to be bilingual, the presence of another language in the family provided me with an understanding of the nature of language itself and of the benefits of multilingualism. I also became aware of some of the subtle differences within languages. For example, although both my parents spoke German there were differences in expressions and in vocabulary between Austrian German and German German. Potatoes are *Kartoffeln* in German and *Erdapfeln* in Austrian.

This interest in language was increased through teaching in multi-lingual schools and I gained qualifications which enabled me to specialise in this area. This has been my main area of expertise leading to more responsible posts and to publication in books and professional journals.

Religion and Jewish Identity

I had always known that my parents were refugees and that they came from Jewish backgrounds but had no clear understanding of what this meant. The evidence was in the family name, Hoselitz, which people found hard to pronounce and to spell, in the strange accents and languages that some in my family spoke, and in some of our food and cultural practices. Most of this I accepted without question because it was 'normal' to me and in some ways I was quite proud of being different, for example in the food that we ate, but in other ways found it mildly irritating and embarrassing as a child although I did not seriously suffer from teasing or ridicule.

Ours was a firmly secular household. My parents were atheists, or as my mother insisted, agnostic, because one 'couldn't know if there was a God', and keen to assimilate. We attended neither church nor synagogue and were not part of the local Jewish community, although they subscribed to the AJR all their lives. We celebrated Christmas but none of the Jewish festivals, in a non-religious fashion, with a tree and presents. Although we had a menorah it was purely for decorative purposes and was never lit. Neither did we have anything approaching a kosher diet. We ate pork and bacon as well as shellfish and would have cream and meat at the same meal. My father was interested and knowledgeable about wine and would certainly not have restricted himself to kosher wine. We had some different food from our friends, such as goose rather than turkey at Christmas and stollen rather than traditional Christmas cake.

My favourite dinner for many years was frankfurters and sauerkraut, which must have been quite difficult to find in the suburbs of Sheffield. I remember being surprised when I went to stay with a friend and was served spinach. My mother cooked very appetising spinach and I could not understand how the vegetable could be made so inedible.

It was clear from an incident in the early 50s that my mother in particular was keen not to be identified as of German origin. We took a family holiday in France and picked up a hitch-hiker who turned out to be German. I was somewhat embarrassed when my mother stared to speak to him in German but with a fake 'English' accent.

In 1958 we took our first family holiday in Germany, Titisee, and Austria, Millstättersee. I sensed that this was a bit of an experiment for my parents to find out how they would react to a return to their countries of origin, which they no longer thought of as home. We stayed in small guesthouses and every evening after supper my brother and I would have to go round all the adults individually and say *'Gute Nacht'*, which we found very embarrassing.

Looking back, I think the holiday also confirmed for my parents that Britain was now their home. This became particularly evident when they subsequently took a trip to the United States, partly to see my uncle and his family in Chicago but largely because Kurt had been offered a job there. It was clear to me when they returned that my mother was not at all keen to make the move. One of her main objections, as far as I could gather, was that in the States it was necessary to declare a religious affiliation, a step which she felt could pave the way for antisemitism. My uncle, who had married a non-Jew, had 'become' Episcopalian, a fact which I later saw as a betrayal of his heritage.

Later I went with my father to Vienna and he took me round many of the places where he had grown up. Both these trips felt uncomfortable at times. I remember my revulsion at the loden jackets, dirndl skirts and pheasant-feathered hats that were prevalent even in urban areas and retain an unreasonable distaste for 'folksiness'. In my late teens I decided to try to improve my German and spent some weeks with a German family in Hamburg, but none of these trips genuinely reconciled me to my German/Austrian background and since then we have rarely spent time in either Germany or Austria.

As a teenager I began to test the boundaries of my Jewish identity. In secondary school I went through a brief religious phase and joined a group of Jewish girls who absented themselves from Assembly. I did not understand the rituals that they practised nor the words that they spoke in their prayers.

In summer 1964 I went to Israel. I visited some of my relatives there and spent several weeks on a kibbutz. I also travelled around the country with a girl I had met on the journey from the UK and saw at first hand the working and living conditions of the Israelis and the Arabs who lived there. I was frequently asked whether I was Jewish and found this difficult to answer since I associated being Jewish with a religion that I did not espouse. But the energy and commitment of the young Israelis I met inspired me and I determined to return after I had finished university. I never did.

In both my parents' families it had been expected that they would meet and marry Jews. On the contrary, when I dated a Jewish boy at university my mother later confided to me that my letters sometimes alarmed her and made her worry that I might marry 'into the faith'. I did not. But I was sufficiently interested in religion as an institution to take the Sociology and Religion option at university and engaged in long conversations with my parents about religion. My father and I both agreed that we were atheists. My mother, who had found a belief in God a great comfort as a teenager, found it more difficult to retract and remained an agnostic. I continue to be interested in the power of religion in society while being deeply critical of some of its manifestations.

Conclusion

Now, at 75, I still ask myself; what does it mean to be a Jew if you are not religious, reject much of what the Jewish state of Israel appears to represent and have no distinctly Jewish culture? I do not seek out specifically Jewish gatherings or societies and do not feel that it is a significant part of my identity. And yet, if asked, I will say that I am Jewish and would hope that if necessary I would 'stand up and be counted'. So, my answer to the Jewish question is still, 'I don't know.'

But I want my children, who are married to non-Jews and have a gentile father and do not think of themselves as Jewish, to know and understand something about part of their family history. I want to honour my parents and their memory. I want, through their experiences, to have greater understanding of discrimination, persecution and prejudice, all of which I have fought against for most of my life. I want people to have an insight into what it feels like to be a refugee. My parents were dislocated and forced to adopt a new country and home. But they embraced what they saw as the equality and lack of prejudice that they found, for the most part, in Britain and although they thought about settling in other parts of the world, when this became possible they actively decided to live in the UK. I want British society to be worthy of that choice.

Chapter 9   My Challenge

Janet Leifer

It is a difficult challenge for me to work out the impact of being a child of refugees on my life. My parents were Jewish refugees from Germany. Unlike many of their relatives and friends they managed to escape the Holocaust, but they were deeply affected by the loss of family and friends. My parents are certainly important, and their memory is very precious to me. Other people who I have shared my life with are also very dear to me and have affected how I have lived my life – my husband, my children and their children and wider family and friends. It is impossible to separate one's past experiences from one's present existence – present and past are inescapably entangled.

David Grossman, talking about the state of Israel, in an article on Amos Oz (Guardian, 5 January 2020) reflects my perception of the Holocaust, 'A vibration of an age-old memory and of unbearably hard traumas that still have not been digested or truly understood.'

There are inexplicable black holes in my family history. It is impossible for me, who has not lived through the Holocaust, to fully comprehend the trauma. I feel a great sense of loss and sadness which I am sure my parents felt, but for me the journey back into their past experiences is difficult, mysterious and precarious.

I have numerous documents, memoirs and photos that relate to my family's life from the 1930s onwards and somewhat unreliable memories of past conversations. I knew most of my family members who survived the Holocaust and was close to some of them. However, this is not the same as sharing their lived experience of the Holocaust and how it changed their lives. As hard as I try it is not as real to me. Whatever happened to them is shrouded in an unknown, terrible horror for me.

Where do I come from?

My parents arrived in Britain in 1939. They were Jewish refugees from Leipzig. The Koenig family (my father's family) business was aryanised by the Third Reich. They had lived a comfortable life. They employed staff including a cook, a maid, and a chauffeur. My grandfather loved classical music and played the piano. This love was shared by his wife and their children.

The Wolle family (my mother's family) arrived in Leipzig in 1901 from Poland, or 'White Russia', as my mother called it. She was the only child born in Germany. Her father, Hirsch Wolle, made a living buying and selling. Her parents were orthodox Jews, speaking Yiddish and her mother, Chava, wore a *sheitel* or wig. My mother was determined to be a modern independent young woman and insisted on going out to work, refusing the idea of an arranged marriage.

My mother arrived in London not knowing what had happened to her father and six siblings (two brothers, four sisters), their spouses and children. She did not speak much English and did not like working as a maid, although being offered employment by Maynard Keynes had saved her life. My father spent most of the war as a private in the Pioneer Corps in the Orkneys.

The 1940s was the start of a new phase in the life of my parents. In Britain they had a chance to start a home and make a secure life for me and for themselves. At the same time, they had suffered great losses and were trying to re-establish links with family and friends who might not have survived the war. After I was born, my mother stayed at home to look after me and our home. I felt much loved by my parents and they always did their best to ensure I felt safe and secure. I grew up in a loving home, was well educated and encouraged to learn about my Jewish identity and also to value and be part of the wider community.

We were members of the South London Liberal Synagogue in Streatham. It took two buses to get there. We did not attend services every week, but always at Rosh Hashanah and Yom Kippur and sometimes the communal Seder at Pesach. I attended the Hebrew classes until the age of sixteen, but my knowledge of Hebrew was quite limited. However, I enjoyed the company of my classmates, whom I continued to see at the Youth Club.

As I grew up, I had a strong awareness of being Jewish. Although I do remember that when I started in primary school some of my classmates said 'You are Jewish' in a way that made me feel it was not good to be a Jew. I had never been called Jewish before, so I said most emphatically that I was not a Jew. It took me a long time to realise that my parents spoke English with an accent, as did relatives and friends. I remember that after a parents' evening at secondary school some pupils said there were some 'continental' parents who attended, and it dawned on me that they were talking about my parents.

By the end of the 1960s both my parents had died. I know that neither of them wanted to visit Germany after the war. My mother would never speak German in public, especially not to German officials dealing with her restitution claim and not even in Italy when we visited northern Italy where German was better understood than English.

The Holocaust cast its shadow over my parents' lives. My mother lost her parents, three sisters, two brothers, one niece and one nephew. I have always felt that there were holes in my life where those who perished should have been. Grandparents, aunts, uncles and cousins I should have known. I was fortunate to know my mother's sister and her husband who managed to flee to France and my cousins, two of her nephews and a niece survived concentration camps. We were always close to those relatives who survived even though they lived abroad.

My father's close family managed to flee to England and his twin brother survived the war in France and settled there. The relationship with my father's relatives was less close for family reasons, but as I have grown up, I have become closer to my cousins especially as we have explored our family history together.

It is very difficult for me to fully comprehend what my parents and their families experienced. I have lived a reasonably secure life and have not had to face the horrors and loss that they faced. However, I do feel that there has always been a big rift in my family history, a loss that can never be redeemed.

When my parents told me about their life growing up in Germany they talked with affection about family and friends. They enjoyed their lives and I do not think it would have occurred to them that they would become stateless refugees.

Who am I?

I am a seventy-four year old widow who has lived most of my life in London, where I still live. I am a mother of two sons and a stepmother and have three granddaughters and one grandson. Having retired from work as a school librarian four years ago, I keep myself busy doing things I enjoy – going to art galleries, the cinema, the theatre, eating out and drinking coffee in agreeable places and playing bridge.

I volunteer at the Jewish Museum in Camden and in the library of the Alpine Club. I took a Masters degree in Library and Information Studies and have always worked in libraries. Since my childhood, I have been fascinated by documents and photos from the past. Family memoirs and photos draw me into the lives of loved ones who are no longer here.

My family history interests me and I would like to pass on a record of this to my sons. I have written some of my recollections with photos of past and present generations. I am delving into Jewish archives and historical archives of Leipzig, where my parents were born and thoughts inevitably turn to the Holocaust.

I have always felt part of the Jewish community, even if my Jewish identity is a little hazy. I am a member of a synagogue but do not attend regularly. For many years I worked in a Jewish school and now I volunteer in a Jewish museum. Consciously or not, I have chosen to be involved in Jewish life and this involvement matters to me.

For most of my adult life I have been interested in politics. At the moment I am involved in a local campaign to protect public services in the London Borough of Barnet with special emphasis on adult social care. This often feels like tilting at windmills but I believe that everyone's wellbeing is important and needs protecting.

My childhood home had a continental atmosphere, I have always enjoyed German (and Austrian) food and drink. To this day they bring back fond memories of my childhood. My father took great pleasure in eating well. At home some of our dishes had a middle European flavour – goose and red cabbage at Christmas, sweet and sour cabbage stuffed with mincemeat, sauerkraut, German sausage – *teewurst, leberwurst*, pickled herring and smoked salmon as well as traditional English food like roast beef.

My family's favourite eating place was Schmidt's Restaurant in Charlotte Street, not far from Goodge Street in central London. This was an institution for lovers of German food and émigrés from Europe. I am reasonably fluent in the German language and have visited Germany and yet…. there is an uneasiness.

I feel guilty about visiting Germany, but I have still done so, visiting Frankfurt and its surrounds (where a longstanding German friend lives) and Berlin and Leipzig, the town where my parents lived and which I find attractive and interesting. The places where I feel the most uncomfortable are at memorials to the former German Jewish communities – spaces where synagogues once stood, Jewish museums, memorials to the holocaust. The memorials are worthy and sincere attempts by Germany to come to terms with the destruction of its Jewish communities, but for me they are soulless places that do not reflect the vibrancy of the communities which were destroyed.

I do not wish to reclaim German citizenship despite the possibility of obtaining an EU passport. I am convinced my parents never wanted to have German citizenship given back to them. I feel if one is a citizen of a country this may give you certain rights (not sure exactly what one would gain from becoming a German citizen if one was not working/ living in Germany) but as a citizen of a country one also has certain obligations and should perhaps contribute to life in that country, something I do not see myself doing in Germany. I do not intend to apply for a German passport but I would help my sons to do so if they wished.

The Holocaust continues to haunt me. I remember my parents going through a long drawn out restitution claim with West Germany. They talked about it in German and I often heard the words '*Rechtsanwalt*' (lawyer) and '*Anklage*' (legal action). I also remember the numbers tattooed on the arms of relatives who had been in concentration camp. As I grew older, I was shocked by the stories of what had happened to my parents' families, especially those who had not escaped the Third Reich in time. As these things happened before I was born, I never met those who perished and never knew the full story of what the survivors had gone through.

My awareness of the Holocaust was partly gained through where my family lived. In our block of flats there was a family of Jewish refugees whom we were friendly with. They had a grown-up daughter with Downs syndrome, so she was especially lucky to have survived the Nazi regime. There was also another neighbour whom I did not really know. She sometimes could be seen running around wildly. She was a Holocaust survivor. As a child I found her behaviour quite scary. I am shocked when I learn about the experiences of Holocaust survivors. I feel that what they have endured is unimaginable.

I have always been interested in languages perhaps because our family and friends spoke a variety of European languages. At university I studied European Studies majoring in French. Throughout my professional life I have had to use foreign languages. To speak to our relatives, it was useful to speak German and French as well as English and Yiddish. My father's relatives all spoke English well. Grosmui, my father's mother, called us the English family, because my parents spoke English to me and perhaps she did not approve of this, although they also spoke in German to each other.

Where am I going?

Recollecting the past is important to me. I like to think about my connection to my parents, my husband, my family and friends and recall our life together. The tradition of naming children after relatives no longer alive appeals to me – I am glad to be named after my grandmother – names that bind one generation to the next. My family, past and present, is very dear to me. I hope I will always feel close to my sons, stepson and their families.

My mother and I experienced a great loss when my father died at the age of 56 in 1961. Sadly, my mother died in 1968. By the age of 22 I had lost both my parents, which I found difficult to cope with and I really missed being part of a family. There is no doubt that this experience made me really value the importance of family life.

It is also impossible for me to forget the impact of the Holocaust on my family. I think it is important to remember what happened to my parents' generation and to talk about it. When I am in the Jewish Museum in Camden, I can see the valuable work that is done with schools in workshops about the Holocaust and the impact it has on participants, some of whom have little or no contact with Jews in their daily lives. Long may it continue. At the same time the suffering of other people living in terrible circumstances around the world must be addressed.

In my lifetime I have encountered antisemitic prejudice, but not on anything like the scale that my parents had to face. Antisemitism should always be challenged. There is no doubt that it exists today however it can be entangled with the struggle between Israel and the Palestinians leading to heated debates and intransigence. One consequence is rifts in the Jewish community, with deep divisions in families. I find it quite distressing that it can be impossible to have an honest, open and civilised conversation between Jews and also between Jews and the wider community. I would like to feel this could be changed and that we could at least talk openly and respectfully without treating each other like bitter enemies.

I would like to think that I can feel empathy for other people who have to endure racist abuse and perhaps this is a topic I should engage with more. It is possible to live quite close to communities who are being abused because of their ethnicity or religion without realising what they are being subjected to. Of course, I know that I cannot keep going forever, but I hope I can be independent and self-reliant for as long as possible, enjoying the company of family and friends and the wider community and remembering past times.

Connecting to the Zeitgeist

I feel that I live in a fast moving, rapidly changing and sometimes exciting world facing challenging issues such as social inequality, poverty, gender identity, climate change and other environmental issues. In some ways quite different from the 1930s and 1940s but with some disturbing similarities such as intolerance, racism, antisemitism, social deprivation and poverty, the rise of political extremism, political unrest and violence.

Since 2010 I have viewed with dismay and anger the destruction of public services in Barnet. It is hard for local authorities to manage finances and deliver public services. The decision makers in Barnet Council decided to pass their responsibilities to others and privatise as much as they could, making a hard to manage situation impossible to manage in a responsible way. Barnet residents with the least clout, disabled residents in need of social care and residents in social housing, have had their lives turned upside down as Barnet Council ignores its responsibility to them. I have joined with other residents in campaigning for fair and proper treatment for residents and Council employees in the campaign group Barnet Alliance for Public Services.

Finishing this chapter in the midst of the Coronavirus pandemic, these are in their own way daunting times. Despite all our difficulties there are signs of community spirit, a desire to help our neighbours and young people's determination to make our world a better place, so we should never give up hope for a better tomorrow.

Chapter 10   The impact of an exile/émigré background

Ines Newman

Introduction

I have operated on the boundaries of academia and political activism. I originally trained as a town planner and then moved into community development and advocacy in London Docklands. Later I was to become a local economic development officer, trying to reduce unemployment, poverty and exploitation in work and improve career development. I ended my career focussing on local government policy, ultimately moving to the local government unit at Warwick University. The link between these career directions was my concern to address disadvantage both through policy development, and practical programmes and political involvement. In reflecting on why this was important to me, it is difficult to disentangle the fact I was an immigrant, the influence of the 1960s and the role of the family. Parents are the main influence on one's values. So, to what extent did my parents' exile/émigré experience impact on my life?

My mother and father would never have met, let alone married without the rise of Nazism in Europe in the 1930s. My mother, Lisl Hollitscher, was a graduate and social democrat from Vienna. My father, Hans Oppenheimer, came from the provincial town of Stuttgart in Germany. He left school at 16 and was a conservative and an entrepreneur. Yet they had a happy marriage and shared many values.

My mother's father, Wilhelm Hollitscher, was the first generation to be able to take advantage of full citizenship rights granted to Jews in the Austro-Hungarian Empire in 1868. He grew up as a religious Jew in poverty in a small village in Moravia. He was able to gain a doctorate in engineering and rose to become the Chief Engineer for the First Danube Steamboat Shipping Company in Vienna. As Stephan Zweig says, Vienna was a city of music and tolerance and you were not truly Viennese without a love of culture. Wilhelm became Vice President of the Vienna Singing Academy, a mixed choir founded in 1858 and conducted by Brahms in 1863.

Lisl, his daughter, was born in 1909 and was independent minded and much more radical than her father. She had no interest in religion, joined the social democrat party and started to travel just before she became 19. She went first to the University of Nancy to get a *Diplôme d'études françaises* and then travelling to England where she was a governess to two girls in Cornwall and then a teacher in a small school in rural Lincolnshire. She returned to Vienna to do a law degree.

However, 1930 saw antisemitic riots in the University and it would not have been a welcoming atmosphere (Neurath, republished 2015). She started going to Alexandria in 1931, financing her trips by writing articles about life in Egypt for the *Neues Wiener Tagblatt*. By 1932 Dollfuss was in power, Hitler came to power in Germany in 1933 and 'red Vienna' was smashed in 1934. Lisl started taking practical courses in gymnastics and beauty and cosmetics from September 1933 and in April 1935 decided to emigrate to Alexandria and to make a living using her skills in beauty treatments and teaching German and gymnastics.

Meanwhile Hans had already been in Egypt for six years. He was a descendant of a family of cattle traders who lived in a small village Ernsbach, near Stuttgart. His father had similarly taken advantage of emancipation and had qualified as a doctor in Munich in June 1894. He had then set himself up as a children's doctor in Stuttgart. He would have had ambitions for his son but Hans was not academic and left school at sixteen. He worked as an intern for a year in Paris and three months in England and then early in 1929, when he was 20, he decided to go to Alexandria to work for his uncle who had a small steel stockholding and cotton and steel trading company in Alexandria. At this stage he was very much an economic migrant. Before the crash, 1.25 million people were unemployed in Germany. By the end of 1930 the figure had reached nearly 4 million, 15.3 per cent of the population. By 1932 over 30 per cent of the German workforce was unemployed. Trade in Egypt was however blooming in 1929/30 and his uncle needed his help.

His mother died a year after he left Germany and his father died six months later, so by 1931 he had lost his main ties to Germany and his future depended on his success with his uncle. He worked very hard, ten-hour days, six days a week and had almost no social life. By 1933 he had broken with the Germans in Alexandria whom he saw as Nazis. He was not a religious Jew and had no links with the significant Jewish community. It was very difficult for a European man to socialise with Arabs, particularly Arab women. He socialised with a couple of young English men but had little in common with them.

One can hear in his letters the delight at meeting Lisl and they soon moved in together getting married in April 1936. Lisl had wanted to get married in a synagogue in order to avoid becoming German. But this did not work out because the Austrians didn't want to give her a passport with the name Oppenheimer if she married in the synagogue. Without a passport in her married name, they were concerned that if they went to Europe for a honeymoon she may not have been able to get a visa to get back to Alexandria. So, they bit the bullet and married at the German Embassy, after having to prove that Hans was a full Jew with his parents' wedding certificate. Eventually this marriage at the German Embassy was important evidence for me in claiming German nationality.

Living in Alexandria during the war was not straightforward, particularly around the El Alamein battle in 1942, but it was a much better place to be than continental Europe. Then in 1948 there was the first Arab-Israeli War and Hans was arrested and put in prison for one night on a trumped up charge. Immediately he was released he applied for the family to emigrate to the UK, Australia or America. The lesson of the last war was that you got out of a county where you faced discrimination and antisemitism as soon as possible.

I have always been relieved that the British visa came through first and the family moved to Bickley, at that time at the edge of London in Kent, in spring 1949. I was eighteen months old. We had various relatives who lived around Petts Wood and Bickley, including Martin Bunzl, a double first cousin of Lisl's mother who had helped relatives, including Lisl's father, to get to the UK in 1939. Lisl's father had died in 1943 but the area was still that with the most family ties in the UK. My parents bought a house in Orpington, Kent and we settled into our new life.

Orpington was not a centre of immigration. I went to Bromley High School where there were no religious Jews or Asian or Afro-Caribbean immigrants. Everyone had names like Jane Smith and I remember teachers coming up to me saying 'Oh, so you're Ines Oppenheimer!' The first time I entered a synagogue was when I got married. I was given no knowledge about Judaism and very little about the Holocaust. I knew my aunt's husband had been captured in France and murdered in the Holocaust but no more details until I studied history at school. My brother and two older sisters had been sent to an English school in Alexandria so already spoke English but we switched from German as the household language to English being our day-to-day means of conversation. The aim was to assimilate as quickly as possible.

In this context it is interesting to ask what it meant to be a refugee. My parents were not refugees in the traditional sense of the word, in that they had not been forced out of Egypt and did not see themselves as victims. But they had faced discrimination in two countries. If the Nazi regime had not come to power in 1933, my father would probably have returned to Germany and my mother would never have left Austria. Her mother was deported and shot on arrival in Kaunas County, Lithuania on 29 November 1941 aged 56 and several cousins who remained in Vienna were murdered during the war.

Living in Egypt was tough on my mother's health. She had two bouts of typhoid, nearly dying both times and this, together with her last pregnancy with my younger sister Susan, made her susceptible to stomach cancer which finally killed her in 1954, aged only 45. But she had loved Egypt: the sun, the sea, the outdoor life and the cosmopolitan community. As she said, she would rather have been a European in Egypt than a Jew in Austria. Fear however drove them out in 1949 and, had they stayed, they would have been forced out in 1956. So, they were both exiles and émigrés.

All this had a set of implications. Firstly, we arrived in Britain in 1949 stateless as my father had had his German nationality withdrawn in 1941. The wish to get British nationality partly explains the obsession with assimilation. In 1955 we had a visit from the immigration officer. As a seven-year-old, I remember how seriously this was taken and being told that we must be on our best behaviour. The official was given a traditional tea with cucumber sandwiches in our garden: we rarely drank tea and never had cucumber sandwiches.

Secondly my father remained nervous that we would be moved on again. He set up trusts in various countries ensuring some of his funds were safely tucked away for the next emergency. This had nothing to do with tax avoidance but reflected his insecurity. We spent time after his death closing all these accounts.

Thirdly both our parents were very aspirational for us children. As children we all knew we were expected to work hard and do well at school. There was no gender distinction, after all my mother was already a graduate and my father's sister also had a degree. Hannah, my eldest sister, who arrived in the UK aged twelve, went on to get into Oxford University to study Modern Languages. The rest of us were meant to follow her. Many immigrant families push their children academically and this can have both positive and negative effects. I made it to Oxford and no doubt this bought some advantages in my career, but I felt completely out of place at Somerville College which was dominated by upper class, very English young women, from private boarding schools. I felt I shared nothing with them in terms of ethnicity or class.

And this brings me to the next point. Despite the attempt to assimilate, the first time I felt English was when my husband, Mike, and I with our two young children went to spend a year in Bordeaux. Early on, we were invited out for a meal with the University faculty. The professor sat at the top of the table and then we were seated in hierarchical form with us at the bottom of the table with a nice young Quebecois couple who were also spending a year attached to the university. The main conversation was all about wine and I had nothing to contribute. I started to realise that I had absorbed more of English culture than I had realised.

Up to that point, despite our family attempts to assimilate, we were categorised as foreigners rather than refugees.

Firstly, there was language and although English was the spoken language, we spoke it as foreigners. Not only were there the obvious accents of my parents but mistakes were made, so even in my twenties I would say: 'I'm fed up of it' or 'that car coming against us' and our sentence structure was often Germanic. Being dyslexic (before dyslexia was a known condition), this particularly impacted on me and I accepted the role of 'entertainer' making my fellow school students laugh at the way I expressed myself. Then there was food. We had an Italian nanny who had joined the family in Egypt before the war and emigrated with us to England. She was a fantastic cook and my mother was a great cake maker. I could not cope with school meals or the cooking of many of the mothers of my friends. My best friend at school had a mother who could cook and this no doubt consolidated the friendship.

We were also 'different' because we ran an open household. Although it was common to have what children now call 'a play date' or to play in the street, it was rare in Orpington in the 1950s to have people staying in your house from all over the world or lots of dinner parties. Households were atomised in their suburban environment. In contrast, not only were we a large family with five children but the house was always full of relatives and friends. Those of my parents' generation always reverted to German, so there was both Italian and German spoken in the household. I remember in my teens going on holiday to Korcula, Yugoslavia with my aunt who lived in Paris and spoke French to her dog and German to my father.

Then there was our nanny to whom we all spoke in Italian. Then a cousin of my mother's who also spoke German to my father and my aunt, but English to us children, and finally Sydney Arrobus, an English painter from Hampstead, who also joined us and only spoke English. I could see the other occupants of the hotel watching us in puzzlement and trying to work out our relationships. We were clearly not a 'normal' English family.

There are various ways children react to these contradictions of pressure to assimilate and the impossibility of doing so. Some of these differences may be gender related. My brother was sent away to an English public boarding school when he was thirteen. This was partly because my parents believed that a boy could not grow up with four sisters. It was also because my mother was ill and my father was struggling to cope with five children. But the key driver was the imperative to assimilate. This was very traumatic for my brother. But he reacted by trying to become even more assimilated. For example, he wanted to be confirmed and played with changing his name from Oppenheimer to Oakland.

In contrast I embraced my difference. There was no way I could ever have married a pure Englishman. I always sought out rebels and 'odd' eccentric people as friends and finally found Mike, a British Jew with a religious mother and atheist father, who satisfied my need to be different without being an observant Jew. The extent to which my left-wing politics are a result of my second-generation experience is more debatable. There were conflicting influences in the family with my left liberal mother and conservative father. I was too young to be fully influenced by my mother before she died. But Hannah, my eldest sister became a life-long liberal, Ralph a Fabian, Margaret a centrist Labour party activist, I was left Labour and my younger sister was closer to the Trotskyist wing of the left when young and ended up as a strong environmentalist. So, the need to go further left than our older siblings and the politics of the era may have had more influence than our immigrant status.

What we all shared however was a strong moral code and a concern for the underdog and asylum seeker. We also all remained internationalists and in favour of European integration. Our German father instilled in us a strong sense of 'duty' and guilt if you failed to do your duty. When I first read Lenz's (1968/86) *The German Lesson,* I realised that in cultural terms I was probably bought up more German than English despite my father's dislike of German authoritarianism and desire to assimilate. Unfortunately, in contrast to his support for refugees and asylum seekers and kindness to strangers, my father had also absorbed German racism. This is not the usual story of immigration, but it was a reality and I have since encountered racism among many first-generation immigrants, including more recent BAME migrants.

Although he was not religious, my father believed Jews were the most intelligent ethnic group and made derogatory comments about other ethnic groups, which were very embarrassing to us children. My mother was far less racist and less constrained by 'duty'. She had no interest in material goods and made no attempt to claim reparations. She had no interest in my father's company which must have been difficult for him. But she had also absorbed the sexist attitudes that were prevalent in society and accepted that the 'boy' would work in the family business. Her ambitions for us girls were not material wealth but education and culture and contributing to society. Even as young children we went from Orpington to central London to the theatre and concerts and we were encouraged to read, learn foreign languages and play musical instruments, passions which were not shared by most of our neighbours. Her lack of interest in materialism and her wider concern about society was a strong family influence and was reflected in my wish to work for the voluntary and public sector.

Our parents were also 'second generation', only recently accessing the middle class and education. Our immigrant status meant we were less embedded in English hierarchical class categories. While ultimately clearly middle class, we were less easily identifiable within the class system. My work has involved interaction with working class communities in East London and Harlow and I felt more comfortable with them than with the upper middle class at Oxford. I have, through all my working life and into retirement from paid employment, remain committed to working to counter disadvantage and poverty. While difficult to prove I suspect this does relate to my exile/ émigré background.

Our eldest daughter Kate works in the international development field. This was initially my first choice of career when I completed my degree. I went to the ODI in 1969 to get some careers advice and they succeeded in persuading me that it would be very difficult for a young woman to succeed in this field. I would need to go to Africa for at least a year, they said, where I would face discrimination. This may have been true but in the end I lacked the determination to follow my dreams, having decided to get married and have a family. So I am particularly proud that our daughter has succeeded in this field and strongly carries forward our values. Our second daughter works in arts education and is similarly driven by wanting to improve the lives of those who are disadvantaged. Our son, like many young men, took more risks about his future career when young, moving from jazz to forestry. Then, when he had a family, the need to earn an income caught up with him and he had no opportunity to pursue the creative or environmental career he had hoped for. He may be able to return to his passions later on in life but it confirms my earlier family experience that in this gendered world it is often easier for women to pursue a more ideologically driven life than men.

The Brexit vote caused all the family great sadness. We had shared the assumption of the educated liberal elite that the world was moving forward to greater tolerance and internationalism. To find out that nationalism was still a very active and growing force was frightening, given our history.

I started considering whether or not I should try to reclaim my German nationality. The advantages were not only retaining a European citizenship but also opening up opportunities for the grandchildren. Germany, after all, seemed to have contended with its past in a way that the UK had notably failed to do. We had failed to understand the damage created by our Empire, never addressed such war crimes as the bombing of Hamburg or Dresden, nor really tackled current anti-refugee sentiments. I felt very conflicted. I had grown up full of anti-German prejudice- it was the strongest aspect of my own racism. I tried to imagine what my father would have done in these circumstances. I knew how anti-German he was. He took pleasure when in Germany in breaking the law, for example crossing the road at a red pedestrian light or parking in a no-parking space. When challenged he would gleefully say he did not understand German! Yet despite this he was the ultimate pragmatist and I felt he would have tried to get back his German nationality. In 1956 during the Suez crisis he was threatened with confiscation of his remaining Egyptian business because he was English and so tried to prove he was German. He wrote in a letter:

> I had to prove that I am a German national. I produced a birth certificate and a
> marriage certificate but this is as far as my proof of being a German can go. How

funny it is that in 1939 I was threatened with confiscation of money in Egypt because I was a German, in 1948 because I was a Jew, and now because I am English. How sordid and sorry an affair politics are!

After six months of telling everyone that I was going to apply for German citizenship in order to overcome my reluctance to do so, I finally started the application in the autumn of 2016. It was surprisingly easy and within six weeks of my application, I was a German and European citizen.

So my exile/émigrée status has come full circle, although I do not have Egyptian citizenship despite having been born there. On reflection the turmoil has bought many positives: a strong moral framework; lessons in resilience and independence; a good education; a love of reading and the arts; a purpose to my life; strong internationalism and an ability to move across the English class system and relate to many different types of people. But I look at my eldest sister, Hannah, who shares many of these positives but not my politics. She also considers contributing to society and helping other people as central in her life but remains a liberal.

Being at University in the sixties and exposed to the radical politics of the time has probably had more impact on my politics than my background. Now less than 10% of Jews vote on the left and the Indian community is rapidly following the same trends. An exile/émigré background can make you more of an individualist, concerned with your own personal success as much as it can make you want to support wider internationalism and those worse off than yourself. For those on the left, we need to hold on to the hope that our ability to pass on our values to our children and our actions to influence the future zeitgeist will make a difference.

Chapter 11   Jewishness, Socialism and Feminism – A Journey

Clare Ungerson

Introduction

I was born in 1944. The story goes that my father, being on some kind of inside track at the War Office, became confident, in the spring of 1943, that Britain and the Allies would win the war. My parents' Jewish baby would not be threatened by the Third Reich so it was safe for my mother to become pregnant. I was to be an only child. By the time I was born my parents' marriage had basically ended in all but name – my father had, from 1941 onwards, embarked on a series of affairs and had often broached the subject of separation with my mother. It took many decades for this situation to resolve itself – they only finally separated in 1976, my father remarrying twice while my mother remained single till she died thirty years later in 2006.

As a consequence of being an only child both my parents poured their personal hopes and frustrations into me - my father wanted me to be very clever (he believed in hereditary IQ and hence my notional intelligence would demonstrate his own) and my mother wanted me to be very beautiful, not look Jewish (there was a constant battle about my hair and weight, both of which were and are quintessentially Jewish) and not marry a Jew. As a child I was able to deliver to my father - I managed to present him with various academic achievements of which he was extremely proud. (I was a foundation exhibitioner at St Paul's Girls' School in London, and I was an undergraduate at the University of Oxford, where I read Philosophy, Politics and Economics.) I was later able to satisfy some of my mother's requirements, marrying someone whose name (Irvine-Fortescue) and Scottish landed gentry ancestry amply fulfilled the wishes of her own parents. I was vaguely aware at the time of our wedding that I was giving her an enormous present. That said, he and I have been happy together, possibly because, much to my mother's disappointment, we have no children.

Given this parental and marital context, how could I possibly emerge as either a socialist or a feminist or a combination of the two? The answer lies, as I will suggest in this essay, very substantially in the fragile Jewish identity of both my parents, and in the pre-Holocaust experience and its ongoing consequences for my mother and those of her extended family who also managed to get away from Germany to Britain. That is not to deny my own agency in my journey to socialist feminism, but, as I will suggest here, there is a clear route from my parents' values to my own.

How my parents Bernard Ungerson and Annelis Gumbel met

My mother, Annelis, had been a student of Art History at the University of Munich for a year when, in 1934, all the Jewish students at the University were told they could not re register for the following year. As a consequence, her very well off parents (her father had been a successful lawyer, her mother along with her aunt owned the Bank of Heilbronn), who lived in the middle of Stuttgart, dispatched her, first to a 'finishing school' in Lausanne in Switzerland, and then to live with a family in Paris where she looked after two small children. In 1936 she moved to London on, as I understand it, some kind of student visa. She was lucky in that she had a brother, ten years older than her, who had come to London first in 1927. Shocked by the antisemitism he had encountered in Stuttgart (I think he had tried to join the most upper class tennis club there and been rebuffed) he persuaded his father to let him study English law whose common law principles he preferred to the German Roman legal tradition. By 1936 he was a practising barrister with chambers in the Middle Temple, and an income high enough to financially guarantee my mother. It was he who decided she should settle in Bloomsbury close to where he was living and he who decided that she should take the 'Special Entrance' exam to get into the London School of Economics, chosen because it was just along the Aldwych from his place of work. There was no question, apparently, of asking my mother what she wanted to do or to study. It was simply expected that she would go to University and be under the very close wing of her brother. And my mother, at first alarmed by the prospect of reading for a degree in Social Science rather than Art History, simply settled to it.

At that time my mother was, according to her own accounts and those of her oldest friends, charming and beautiful. Her beauty was enhanced by her glamorous clothes which were made for her by her Stuttgart dressmaker. She continued, during the two years of 1936-8, to go backwards and forwards to Stuttgart, often taking her dirty washing with her to be laundered by the faithful Hedwig (too old to be banned from working for a Jewish household) back home. She went on skiing holidays in either Switzerland or Austria each Christmas and Easter, usually with her brother and at least once with a new London girl friend who was also German Jewish. As things grew worse for Jews in Germany and my grandparents increasingly found their property being purloined, she took to smuggling bits and pieces of jewellery out of the country.   She eschewed politics – she thought LSE was a hotbed of German Nazi spies so she kept out of anything remotely controversial and just got on with her work and self enhancement. She made a number of girl-friends, almost all of whom were, like herself, German Jews but none of them, I think, quite as originally well off as my mother. She also had a German Jewish boyfriend whom she had met in Lausanne and they were in London together but only briefly. She was devastated when he decided to emigrate to the United States (despite him being resident in NYC they stayed in touch to the end of their lives. I went with her to his 90th birthday party held in the Orangery of Kensington Palace. He was widowed by then and she was placed in pride of place beside him at the lunch. We sat at a table with, amongst others, William Rees Mogg, father of the dreadful Jacob).

My father was also a student at LSE, two years ahead of my mother. He was Jewish but from an almost completely different background from her. His parents, my paternal grandparents, had arrived in this country from Russia (near Lublin which is now in Poland) in 1911. They brought with them their little son Julius, and, by the time they arrived in the UK, my grandmother was pregnant with my father. Some of my grandmother's family were already here, in particular my great uncle Morris who was working as a tailor in central London. My grandparents settled in Soho, where my grandfather found work as a tailor's presser. My father was born in January 1912. My grandparents spoke Yiddish at home and that was my father's first language. To the end of their lives my grandparents were unable to read. I suspect that they must have had some schooling in Russia but had only learnt to read either the Hebrew script of Yiddish or the Cyrillic script of Russian and when they moved to England they relied, first on their sons, and then on their grandchildren, to shepherd them through the Roman script of English. (When I was a graduate student in London and my grandfather took me out to a restaurant or a concert – which he often did – I had to read the menu or the programme out to him.)

Eventually they had another son, Sidney, and at some point in the 1920s they moved out of London to Westcliff on Sea near Southend in Essex. There they owned and ran 'The White City Restaurant'. I have a wonderful photo of my grandfather standing in the porch of the shop alongside a white coated manager (he always had to have a manager because of the literacy problem) and four waitresses in black and white uniforms. The double fronted shop declares, in elaborate gilt lettering: J.UNGERSON on one side and on the other FISH SNACKS. Quite how my grandparents had managed to put together the money to launch this enterprise is a complete mystery. But they were certainly not short of ambition: by then my grandfather had decided that his oldest son, Julius, was to become a world class violinist (he even hired the Wigmore Hall for Julius to give a concert there) and his second son, Bernard, who was very good at maths, was to become a world class genius. Sidney, their third son, had slight learning difficulties and seems to have been largely left alone – which I think was the reason that, of the three brothers, he was by far and away the most contented and the most happily married (to a wife who also had slight learning difficulties). The White City Restaurant must, in the 1920s, have been very profitable because they managed to send my father to a local private prep school, which is where he learnt to speak English with a perfect toff's accent (neither of his brothers broke away from an Estuary English accent quite as successfully as my father). In the early 1930s my grandparents moved back to London and settled near Blackheath, my father won a scholarship to the local Grammar School and later a scholarship to the London School of Economics (thus demonstrating that he was indeed a genius). My grandfather, having sold the restaurant, bought a business in the Woolwich High Road (which he ran till he was in his late seventies and his manager – the one who could read – died very suddenly in the shop). In 1937 my paternal grandparents had bought, brand new, a tiny bungalow with a large garden in Eltham and lived a suburban life in south east London for the rest of their lives.

My parents, Bernard and Annelis, had two things in common when they met: first, they were both strikingly good looking – their engagement photographs are stunning. But secondly, and far more important in the long run, they both had parents who had rejected most of or all of their Jewish heritage. This was particularly the case with my mother's family. There is no knowing, now, why her parents made strenuous efforts, in late nineteenth century Germany to erase their ethnicity to such an extent that when my mother was born in 1913 they had her christened in a Lutheran church. That said, it was not that unusual; in the early twentieth century the German Jews were the most assimilated in Europe. (When my mother returned to Stuttgart on an AJR organised trip sometime in the 1980s, she went to the main Synagogue in Stuttgart – the first time she had ever been in it – and found her parents' names struck through on the membership list. Notwithstanding her parents' departure from the Stuttgart Jewish community, my great uncle Siegfried Gumbel was, I now know, a leading light in the Stuttgart Jewish community until he was murdered in 1942.) Moreover, my maternal grandparents brought my mother and her brother up to be classic self-hating Jews. Deeply conservative, for them, social class and social status, as laid down by the conventions of German societal norms, trumped ethnicity and loyalty to the Jewish community. My mother often told the story of how her father, on one of their many foreign holidays, would go into a hotel or a restaurant to inspect it before the family descended from their car, and return saying 'No – too many Tyrolese' by which he meant too many Jews. (My mother clearly thought, in her retelling, that this was amusing and retained this epithet to her dying day. She told me, with a note of pride, two days before she died 'I am an antisemite' to which I could only reply 'I know'.) Her brother, who had a lifelong very strong influence on my mother, was determined to marry out, saying that there was a Jewish Problem and the only way to solve it was to intermarry till Jewry disappeared. In the 1950s he did just that, ironically and perhaps inevitably marrying someone with strong organised antisemitism connections (his mother in law was an Empire Loyalist, his brother in law a Conservative MP who belonged to the racist neo Fascist Monday Club.) He never told his children he was German, let alone Jewish, and as he grew older and his children became teenagers he became silent – I always thought it was because he was so worried that one of their friends would recognise his accent or his children would enquire about his own childhood. Eventually, when they were in their late teens, their mother told their two children of their father's origins and told them that neither she nor their father would ever speak of it again and neither should they.

So, in the early 1930s in Germany my mother was well on the way to being 'deracinated' in her own self-perception. She used to tell me, with a mixture of pride and shame, how, in Munich when she was a student, she had been pursued by someone she knew was a Nazi – his great appeal was that he was an aristocrat – until he looked her up on some list of Stuttgart Jews and dropped her like a stone. Her process of assimilation in Germany, and, presumably, her fulfilment of her parents' wish that she marry out was entirely put in abeyance by her emigration to England. Encountering for the first time the intricacies of the British social class system and English xenophobia she made, as far as I know, no 'English' friends in London – only German Jewish ones.   And then she met my father, an English Jew but nevertheless one who, like her, was moving in a similar trajectory. His posh accent, his good looks, his self-assurance and his background (which my mother told me she found, at least initially, 'romantic') intrigued and attracted her. For him too, Jewishness had become a very loose bag from which he was keen to escape. His parents, my Yiddish speaking grandparents, had only in very limited ways brought him up in the Jewish religious tradition.

I very much doubt that my father was bamitzvahed – he never mentioned it if he was – although he was circumcised, I presume as a tiny infant within Jewish liturgy. (The reason I know this is that my mother always told the story that when, immediately after my birth she was told I was a girl, her immediate response was 'Thank goodness!' because she knew there would be no trouble with her in laws about circumcision which she was determined to avoid had I been a baby boy.) I would be very surprised indeed if anything resembling Friday night dinner ever happened in my grandparents' house or that their sons took days off school during Jewish High Days and Holy Days.

However, my grandparents continued to live, in many respects, a very Jewish cultural life - their standard fare was Eastern European, my grandmother's sauerkraut pan had pride of place in her tiny Eltham kitchen, her *apfel strudel* was to die for. In her much later years, when she had senile dementia and was living in a back ward of Bexley Mental Hospital, my grandfather would every day take her her lunch, which usually consisted of what he called 'Viennas' (small German sausages.) Their Jewish cultural commitment really came to the fore when, to their utter horror, their son Julius fell in love with the goy girl next door. There were rows of such volume and – my cousins, Julius's daughters, report – such violence between father and eldest son that my own father, when recounting them once to me, looked shaken by the memory. One aspect of the conflict, according to my father, was that my grandparents went to the local Rabbi to plead with him to help them dissuade their son Julius from his terrible commitment to marrying out. There was nothing the Rabbi could do of course - given that my grandparents had probably never taken their sons to synagogue, the Rabbi was hardly an authority figure in my Uncle Julius's landscape. Julius did eventually marry Jean Fraser the girl next door (and they did not live happily ever after).

As far as the story I am telling here is concerned, there is one explanation for this strangely divided behaviour of my grandparents, and one consequence for Bernard and Annelis. The explanation lies in my grandparents' politics – which they had brought with them from Lublin. *They were Communists.* Uneducated and unread, they believed, with an unalterable fervour, that religion was the opium of the people. In the UK they were members of the British Communist Party which meant that they were never granted British citizenship. In the 1950s when their business in Woolwich began to prosper, they took to going on cruises, always on Soviet ships and always prefaced by a row with my father who had, because they couldn't read, to make the arrangements for their visas (they had something called a 'travel document' each, but no passports so they needed visas for all the countries their cruise ship would be visiting). The row with my father was always the same – they should leave the Communist party and subsequently apply for British citizenship, thus saving him a great deal of trouble. They always refused. Their close family, also living in the UK, all of them from my grandmother's side, had similar politics. My grandmother's brother Morris, my grandmother's sister Kate and most of Morris and Kate's children were also members of the British Communist Party, although in the mid 1950s the children began to peel away and some of them became members of the Labour Party. (One, my father's Cousin Rose, also became a staunch Anglican and the head mistress of a C of E primary school; her brother, Cousin Dave, was active in his Labour party till he died – he had an obituary in *Tribune*.)

The consequence, for Bernard and Annelis, of the row about Julius marrying out was that my father, who, until then had only had gentile girlfriends, decided to try to avoid a similar row. Annelis told me that almost as soon as they met, he told her that his mother had recommended to him that he marry 'a nice German girl' – by which my grandmother had clearly meant a German Jewish refugee girl, many of whom were, in the second half of the 1930s, finding their way to London. Thus two young Jews, both of whom had begun to move away from Jewishness and Jewish identity, came together. Each fitted the other's script. My father remained a bit frightened of his parents, particularly of his mother, but he was ashamed of their ignorance, their illiteracy and their central European culture. My mother was trying, like her brother, to become 'more English than the English', acquire an upper class

English accent and a suitable English husband. She didn't quite make it, but given the way Bernard was shifting his identity, she almost succeeded. For my father, the nice German girl satisfied a short-term problem, although in the long run it was to irk him more and more.

In one important respect my parents remained very different. My father, despite his opposition to his parents' Communism, remained of the left and deeply interested in politics. Like his cousins, he joined the Labour Party. He developed party political ambitions, got himself elected to be Vice President of the National Union of Students, and took an active part in the anti-appeasement campaigns of the late 1930s. In contrast my mother continued her apolitical stance, regarding politics as extremely dangerous territory, and, advised by her brother, steered clear of anything remotely activist. That said, her German Jewish girlfriends, were much more active, two of them involved in left wing politics, one of them to the extent of colluding with her brother and sister both of whom, post war, were unmasked as very important Soviet spies.

My parents married in Marylebone Registry Office in July 1938. There was no question that they should have a Synagogue wedding. My mother's parents did not attend - not because they disapproved of Bernard – they liked him a lot – but they knew that if they left Stuttgart and came to London there was a risk they would be unable to return to Germany. Despite the growing problems they had in Germany they were confident they were safe there – their connections with the Stuttgart legal and financial elite would, they were sure, protect them and anyway they were too old for officials of the Third Reich to bother with them.

Married life in London and the coming of war: my German grandparents' arrival in England

My parents honeymooned in France and Germany and spent time in Stuttgart with my grandparents. On their return to London they settled in Notting Hill, at the Ladbroke Grove end. Not a particularly salubrious part of London, and not particularly near a large Jewish community, the area had the advantage of Victorian houses with large rooms and high ceilings. Their rented flat in Arundel Gardens had two roomy bedrooms and a sitting room and my mother could shop for everything she needed in the nearby Portobello Market. They had a very active social life, often having friends to stay. My mother started a secretarial course at Pitman's college, and taught German to private individuals.

My father was working. After graduating with a degree in Politics and Economics from LSE (not with a first which is clearly what he had hoped for and probably expected) he had gone, as a student, to the National Institute of Industrial Psychology to train to be what was known then as an 'industrial psychologist'. Nowadays this would be called 'Human Resources'. I suspect it was the new scientific rationalism surrounding paid work which drew my father to this discipline. Psychometric testing had recently become the fashion in the theory and practice of industrial and educational psychology. So called 'IQ tests' had been developed which measured the 'intelligence quotient' of an individual. Later, in the post war period, personality tests were also developed. Both methodologies had at their core the idea that heredity was more important than environment in determining intelligence and personality, both of which could be assessed at young ages and remained stable throughout the life course. Proponents of these methods also argued that there were differences in the achievement of social groups, increasingly defined by race but also class, that could be explained by inherited intelligence and marriage within 'gene pools'. My father, with his excellent numeracy and a very strong commitment to empiricism, fell in love with these methods. I suspect the idea that his own biography and that of his highly musical brother, brought up in an illiterate household without a book or newspaper in sight (except for the colourful magazine called 'Soviet Weekly' and an unplayed piano in the lounge), could be explained by inherited genes appealed to him enormously. He did well at the National Institute of Industrial Psychology and very quickly became one of their full-time consultants. The other feature of the training at the NIIP that my father absorbed was the idea of using Time and Motion studies to promote business efficiency. Workers were studied, their movements timed and analysed, and experts devised better and more efficient ways for them to work. My father's first consultancy work in 1938 and into 1939 was to conduct time and motion studies in factories in Manchester and Lancashire. This meant he was away a lot, although in the early years of their marriage my mother quite often accompanied him, staying with him in hotels and guest houses in Nelson and in Barnsley.

My mother kept a daily diary throughout her long life. So far, I have read them closely for the years 1938 to 1942. I now know how often she ran a temperature and what precisely it was, how long she slept in at weekends, how often she visited her German dentist and what precisely he did to her teeth, and, most particularly, how often she saw her friends, her brother and members of my father's family (very often as it happens in the run up to war and during the war). I also know exactly when my father got home from work (often very late) and that he was out singing in a choir or playing chess or 'ping pong' many evenings. What I do not know, because she very rarely mentions it, is her response to what was going on in the world and particularly in Germany where her parents still lived. *Kristallnacht*, for example, does not get a mention although it was very widely reported in the British press. On 9 November 1938 my mother baked some biscuits, on 10 November my paternal grandfather came for supper, on 11 November a German friend came for supper and on 12 November my mother slept till 10am and that evening my parents held a big 'sherry party' for about thirty friends and family. That's it. Although on 14 November 1938 she does note that she wrote a letter to her parents, content unmentioned.

That Christmas, their first as a married couple, my parents travelled by ferry and train to Stuttgart on 24 December. They stayed with my grandparents and visited some of my mother's wider family and some of her friends. My mother says nothing at all in her diary about what she saw in Stuttgart, whether she encountered the Third Reich in any official capacity, whether she saw anything that particularly impressed or alarmed her. On 1 January 1939 they returned, and my mother, writing in English for the first time, notes that 'Train full of refugees, talked to many of them, very depressing'. That is a very unusual comment. My mother's world view – that she and her immediate family were really the only things worth noting – was already writ large. She never ever mentioned her wider German family (her father had been one of many siblings so there must have been masses of cousins) and, in her diaries, there is never any mention of what might have happened to them during the war.

I have always been given to understand that it was over that Christmas holiday in Stuttgart that my father persuaded my maternal grandparents, aged in their late sixties, to leave Germany. They had been deeply reluctant to go but the steady drip drip of confiscation of their property, the compulsions of stating Jewish identity, the change of their names to include 'Israel' for my grandfather and 'Sara' for my grandmother – particularly when they had tried so hard not to be Jewish – must have made it possible for my father to push on an open door. Something must have been put in train because, almost exactly six months later, on 10 June 1939, my maternal grandparents arrived in this country. My mother's diary entry reads as follows:

> Parents arrive at Victoria at 9.10. We fetched them, also Daddy [my paternal grandfather], and drive them home. Aunt Ida [my German grandmother's sister who was already in London] here from half 12 onwards. Lunch. Aft. Lerses [my mother's

cousins Rudolph and Albrecht – Ida's sons] here till 4. Walter [my mother's brother] here till half 10. Mother looks ill.'

My Oma and Opa had arrived in England with 10 marks each and a very large trunk (which I finally disposed of in 2006 when I cleared my mother's flat). In London, given that their immediate family was entirely assembled there, they were far from alone. And yet – and I find this rather strange – my mother and her brother had already arranged for them to stay, for three months, in a guest house in Bournemouth where they knew no one and had no family connections. It's possible that this was all the family could afford and that guest houses in London were too expensive (although most refugees did find somewhere to live in London, at least initially.). Maybe it was a strenuous effort, on my Uncle Walter's part, to keep his parents away from other Jews, even from the very beginning. Or, more benignly, my mother and uncle thought that, if their parents spent three months by the seaside over the summer months of 1939, their parents would construe it as just another long foreign holiday. Eight days after their arrival in this country my father drove my grandparents to Bournemouth. As my mother recorded for that day: 'Mother cries when we leave. Dreadful. Back home at 10'.

My mother always told me that the very next day my Opa, determined to become a properly informed conservative Englishman, bought the *Times* newspaper and slowly but surely, through this somewhat heavy going medium, began to teach himself English. But they had not left Germany and the humiliations of the Third Reich entirely behind. Their 'Exemption from internment' cards, gives their Bournemouth address and gives their names as 'Sigmund Israel Gumbel' and 'Lilli Sara Gumbel'. They had not, yet, dared shed the deeply personal change the Nazis had imposed upon them.

War and Post War

Between the outbreak of war in September 1939 and late 1941 my father continued to work for the NIIP as a consultant. Most of his work was concerned with time and motion studies in factories in Lancashire and Yorkshire; this was, apparently, a 'reserved occupation' which meant he avoided conscription. At the height of the Blitz his entire new German family – my mother, my Opa and Oma and my great aunt Ida (her sons Rudolph and Albrecht were interned at the time) – went to live with him for some months in a small house in Barnsley, Yorkshire. This must have been a great strain – Aunt Ida was, according to my mother's diary, 'hysterical ' a lot of the time – but both my parents remembered it as a good time and the last time when their marriage was properly happy.   My mother's diaries also make it clear that my father was increasingly thinking of enlisting, and his own father was also minded that he should join the British Army. She was very alarmed at this prospect and determined that he not become a fighting soldier. My father's NIIP contacts began to work for him and in November 1941 the perfect army job materialised: an appointment to the Directorate for the Selection of Personnel which was part of the War Office and located in Eaton Square in London. His entry rank was as 'Captain' and my mother noted on November 20, 1941: 'Bernard's uniform arrives from Huddersfield. He tries it on. It's a queer feeling for me to be married to a British officer!'.

My parents had, by mid-November 1941, returned to London.   They had found a flat in Bayswater, in a rather grim block of flats called Ralph Court at the top of Queensway, opposite the Porchester Hall and Porchester baths. This was to be my childhood home until I was eleven; at that age we moved to another rather nicer block of flats located in Notting Hill. Ralph Court was not at all suitable for a child. The flat was small (two bedrooms with a tiny kitchen), it was on the third floor of a seven storey block. There was no open communal space. As I grew older, I disliked it more and more. When I asked my mother how we had come to be living there she always had the same explanation: there were lots of flats available in 1941 due to people leaving London because of the Blitz. As refugees and Jews they had few contacts in the London suburbs which were relatively safe (not true because my father's family were all living in suburban south east London). There was a general belief that a flat on the middle floors of large block was the safest place to be – in the event of a direct hit the middle floors were the safest (I still don't understand why this was the case). Moreover, and this was the main reason why they chose Bayswater, her brother had been very clear that an address near Hyde Park was socially acceptable, even if it was, in his view, 'the wrong side of the park'. Added to this was the fact that it wasn't Hampstead or Golders Green or, heaven forbid, Willesden where large numbers of Jews had settled.

Bayswater was attractive precisely because it was not known to be a particularly Jewish area. (At least it seemed not to be – it was only after I was born in 1944 that my mother discovered that she was surrounded by German Jewish refugee mothers, almost all of whom had had babies at about the same time as her. From 1944-59, when my parents and I left London for Merseyside, her closest friends were that group of mothers, known – of course – as the *Mutterbund*.) I now also know, from a close reading of my mother's diaries, that they quite deliberately chose a small flat because they were determined that Aunt Ida should not continue to live with them. On leaving Barnsley, Ida was packed off to a hotel in Keswick (presumably because she was closer there to her sons who were interned on the Isle of Man) and my Oma and Opa came to live in one of the two bedrooms in Ralph Court. My Opa died in December 1942 (before I was born) and Oma continued to live with us in Bayswater and later

Notting Hill until she died at home, aged 84, in 1957. In the 1950s my mother had become the full-time carer of her and of me.

The war was a very good time for my father. He never saw active service and I don't suppose he ever handled a gun. In his British Army officer uniform he travelled on the tube every morning to his office in Eaton Square. However, within the august confines of Eaton Square, he was fighting his own battles. He was determined to root out the old boy networking that had, until his arrival, been the conventional method for officer selection in the British Army. Men who had been to the 'right' public school, whose fathers before them had been Army officers, found themselves up against a new class of grammar school scholarship boys who were wedded to the scientific tenets of twentieth century business methods. On a daily basis my father engaged in what he considered to be his corner of the class war. His dislike of public school educated men, particularly those who had been to Sandhurst, was laid down in this period and continued to the end of his life. His battles were, I think, relatively easily won. Just as in the current Coronavirus pandemic, the advent of war meant that scientists were able to open up a space where knowledge-based policy making could sometimes trump the traditions of a class based education system. My father's view prevailed, and as IQ testing was rolled out throughout the armed services as the main method of officer selection, so his army career prospered. By the end of the war he was a Major and in 1946 he became a full Colonel. He remained in the Army until 1951 and emerged with a CBE. My mother was thrilled - at last she had acquired the social status that her German upbringing had schooled her for. Her brother, my uncle Walter, continued to call my father 'Colonel Ungerson' well into the 1960s.

My father had also, at this stage of his life, begun to lay the foundations of an academic career. He had published in journals like *Occupational Psychology* and later on, in the 1970s, he published a couple of books. He had also, during the war, made academic friends who were strong proponents of IQ testing, in particular Professor Hans Eysenck of the Institute of Psychiatry whom he seemed to hero worship, and Professor Philip Vernon, an educational psychologist at the Institute of Education. (In 1995 my father, aged 83, married Philip Vernon's widow. She was his third wife; my mother called her 'Mrs Ungerson number 3'.) My father's conversation and assessment of others was increasingly dominated by whether or not they had achieved first class degrees and whether they had gone to Oxbridge – both of which he strongly approved of despite not having done either himself. However, I suspect his new found friends advised him that his army career did not cut the mustard as far as academe was concerned and that he was better advised to go into 'industry'. In fact he went, from the army, into 'retail', becoming a Director of Personnel for major firms such as the Distillers Company, the John Lewis Partnership, Littlewoods Stores and Brooke Bond Liebig. He frequently changed jobs, partly for romantic reasons (to get away from or move towards some liaison or other) but also because, in the boardrooms of these major companies, he kept encountering public school educated men whom he disliked. He could be an extremely rude man and very dogmatic; before long they came to dislike him too and moved him on.

As to his politics, he remained on the left, but only slightly so. He was no longer a member of the Labour Party. We took the *News Chronicle*, the *Observer* and *Reynolds News* as our newspapers, and he belonged to the National Liberal Club. His passionate advocacy of a methodology that has long since been denounced as racist and has become a tool of far right commentators did not embarrass him. That is because he did not accept the logic of that critique. Instead he saw IQ and personality testing as the great liberator from class and race prejudice. He felt these methods countered the social class based exclusion that he had encountered in the army and ensured that the talents of clever working class individuals (like him) would be recognised. Later, he came to believe these methods were neutral in relation to race and hence mitigated what he called 'race bias'. He did put his money where his mouth was and, when we moved from London to Liverpool and he started to work for Littlewoods, he immediately queried why there were no blacks working in Littlewoods stores (he was amazed to be told that there weren't any Catholics either). He acquired a national reputation for fighting for fair selection and, as a consequence, once the legislation was put in place in the 1970s, he was appointed a member of the Equal Opportunities Commission and of the Race Relations Board. He was determined to root out discrimination on the grounds of class, race and sex which he saw as disabling grit in the push to the meritocracy he wanted.

Me: socialism and feminism

It should now be clear where my values spring from. I am my father's daughter in the sense that I have had a lifelong interest in politics and in social justice. My father's interest in equality of opportunity (he was never interested in equality of outcome) and in social improvement through enlightenment encouraged me to think in policy terms. Experience also drove my leftward thinking. My mother's nostalgia for what she presented as the golden years of her Stuttgart childhood compared with my upbringing in the cramped and crowded conditions of Ralph Court, Queensway indicated the essential precariousness of life and the need for generous state intervention when people and individuals are pushed into penury. My paternal grandparents and their descendants' families kept me in touch with Labour party values and, in particular, since some of them stayed in the tailoring trade, with working class people close to home.

Above all, my Uncle Walter and his family kept my anti-Tory sentiment well stoked. He did manage to locate himself on the right side of the park – on marriage to another barrister (he called her his 'English Rose') he bought a house in Knightsbridge (where, almost seventy years later, one of my cousins still lives). His wife became a Conservative councillor on both Kensington and Chelsea council and the Greater London Council. At lunch parties and drinks parties in his house in the 1950s and 1960s I heard racism and social snobbery in casual conversation that entirely took my breath away – and always, with absolute predictability, provoked my father into shouting accusations of Fascism. There were other aspects of experience that were less allied to family and more to our location. Living in Bayswater and then Notting Hill I was well aware, in my early teens, of the growing settlement of people from the Caribbean particularly in the streets at the northern end of Portobello market where we mainly shopped for food. I was very intrigued by the way our neighbourhood was changing, but at the same time was concerned at what I could see of the appalling housing that these newcomers were confined to.

Similarly, when we moved, in 1959, to Merseyside to an area selected by my parents precisely because it had no Jewish population at all, I began to spend time in Liverpool. I fell in love with that city and its people, but at the same time was aware that what I witnessed, as a casual observer, was a grim and grinding poverty such that I had never seen in London. Later, when I had placements in a Liverpool Citizens Advice Bureau and in a Liverpool settlement, I encountered that poverty face to face. Equality of outcome engineered by macro-economic policy and progressive taxation, social protection, decent education for all, and a properly funded and free health service for all seemed to me to be the only answers to the problems and issues I encountered there.

As to feminism, it seemed to fit like a bespoke shoe. My father's ambitions for me had translated into my own ambitions for professional success and my parents' unhappiness together leached into a desire on my part for financial and social independence outside marriage. But it was not until I was working at the Institute of Race Relations in the late 1960s and Sheila Rowbotham came to give a paper on women's oppression that I finally found the voice and the collectivity that I seemed to have been searching for for years. Increasingly I wanted to move away from urban studies where I had been engaged since my postgraduate degree and somehow or other integrate my new-found feminist politics into my research based working life. Taking 'the personal is political' as my lode star, I looked at my own biography, and there, hidden within plain sight, was my mother's care for Oma. That activity had occupied my mother, restricted her, driven a further wedge between my parents, throughout my childhood. There had never been any question of my uncle and his wife taking responsibility for the care of Oma despite their enormous house which contrasted with our cramped circumstances. (That said, they did very occasionally take her on holiday and my uncle did financially contribute to her upkeep.) My interest in an analysis of the gendered process of care was immediately sparked and continued throughout my further academic life. In 1987 I published my first book on care. Entitled *Policy is Personal: sex, gender and informal care,* it was dedicated to both my grandmothers, the one who had been cared for informally at home by my unpaid and unrecognised mother, and the other who had been cared for in an NHS mental hospital, by women nurses with very low status and pay.

It is only with some hindsight that I now recognise that, if it had not been for the Holocaust, my mother would never have been the full time carer of Oma. If she and her parents had managed to stay in Stuttgart, if my mother had married and settled there, it is impossible to imagine that she would have continued to live with her parents. There were enormous sums of money located in that family and my mother and her notional husband would have had ample resources to form their own household away from their original families. The process of care that I observed – and, in my professional life managed to make so much of – had been directly impacted by the fact that we were Jews and had been persecuted by the Third Reich.

Becoming and being a Jew

I have always been clear, despite my parents' efforts to hide it, that I am both Jewish and the daughter and granddaughter of refugees. Growing up in Bayswater within the warm embrace of the *Mutterbund*, all my childhood friends, with not a single exception, shared that heritage. That said, none of us came from observant families and none of us ever went near a synagogue (though some did later as they grew into their teens and wanted to meet other young people like themselves). My sense of Jewish identity came through the prism, not of Jewish liturgy and daily practice but rather through the prism of embarrassment - even shame - and fear. We were always hiding. When we went as a family, including my uncle and Oma, to Germany every summer in the late 1940s and early 1950s, staying in a grand hotel in the Black Forest, spending the restitution money on the assumption that the money would never be allowed out of Germany, no one spoke German if they could possibly avoid it. When I met English people who enquired, as so many did, about the origins of my name, I was instructed by my parents to claim it as 'Scandinavian'. When I went to a secondary school in London where there were so many Jewish girls (many the daughters of German refugees) that there were separate Jewish prayers every morning, my parents made it clear that I was not to go to them – and I didn't, despite being intensely curious as to what happened at them. When I went to secondary school in Birkenhead I continued to go to morning assemblies in the Christian tradition. I observed the one and only Jewish girl at that school enter the school hall after prayers every morning and thought of her as brave but, despite a sense of our affinity, had no desire to join her for fear of antisemitism from my new found friends (not that there was ever the slightest sign of that). At that time of my life, in my late teens and very early twenties, I very rarely mentioned my Jewish heritage, partially because, despite its importance to me, I knew so little about the practice of being a Jew – and, like my parents, was afraid.

This constant theme of denial began to resolve for me when, as a graduate student, I went to the London School of Economics. Suddenly I found myself in the company of other Jewish students, who, looking at me and looking at my name, saw me for what I am. They were comfortable with their Jewish identities and I became much more comfortable with mine. I made, yet again, another set of lifelong friends who were Jews, many observant, and none of them ashamed or in hiding. As I grew older, I became much more open about my origins, always explaining, when asked about my surname, that it was possibly a Yiddish name meaning 'son of a Hungarian'. When I dedicated my first single authored book to my grandmothers, I was aware that, by doing so, I was declaring my Jewish origins to my academic community. When I kept my surname on marriage, I did so knowing that the questions about my origin would keep on coming, and that, as one of the very few Ungersons left after the Holocaust, I was hoping to keep the name alive. As I grew older, I began to recognise my parents' hiding policy as understandable and not that unusual. It was part of their defence against antisemitism and part of their strategy to protect me. Even more recently, particularly as a result of my mother's long period of lonely frailty living independently in a part of

London with many resident Jews, I have realised how that policy all too easily backfired since it separated them from the Jewish community which could have given them the sense of 'home' they both needed.

Eventually, I made my way back into my Jewish and refugee identity by writing a book, in my retirement, about German Jewish refugees who, in 1939, came to live – all 4000 of them - in an old First World War camp on the edge of Sandwich in East Kent. This is the town where I just happen to live. The publication of *Four Thousand Lives: the rescue of German Jewish men to Britain, 1939* (2014, 2019) has been the re-entry point for me. It has taken me to synagogues and Jewish community centres, to Jewish philanthropic organisations, to Jerusalem (and to the West Bank), to Seders and dinners, both formal and informal, where the only non-Jew has been my husband. This experience has been both exciting and occasionally disconcerting. But I am confident that, despite the occasional fierce political difference, there has always, at base, been a welcome precisely because I am a Jew. We have a shared ethnicity, shared ancestral histories and, in many ways, shared personal biographies. And that is deeply comforting.

The Zeitgeist where I live

The Parliamentary Constituency I now live in is South Thanet. Parts of Thanet contain the most deprived wards in the South East; Margate and Ramsgate are classic 'left behind' territory. This is where Nigel Farage, thinking he would be a shoo in, stood as a Parliamentary candidate in the 2015 General Election. The Conservatives' successful counter blast was to field a candidate who, with Farage, had been a founder member of UKIP and stood as a UKIP candidate in other Kent constituencies until he fell out with Farage and joined the Conservative party. Craig

MacKinlay, that Conservative candidate, has been the MP for South Thanet ever since. In the EU Referendum 63.8% of South Thanet voters elected to leave the EU.

Located so close to the English Channel, many local residents regard this part of the world as on the front line of defence against marauding foreigners, who come, in tiny numbers and at enormous risk, across the channel in small boats. The MP for Dover, now a Conservative in a constituency that had a Labour MP in the 2000s, is a regular voice on the local news deploring this migrant arrival and hectoring the French for allowing it to happen. Racism, racist language, racist political activity, Islamaphobia are common currency. in the dim and distant days before lockdown when we could go to the gym, I often heard the respectable ladies with whom I worked out (many of them one time Londoners) quietly express, over a cup of tea after a class, views that made me shiver – and very occasionally (but not often enough), to their utter amazement, I remonstrated. Antisemitism is less overtly expressed but I have heard it, on both right and left, and in casual conversation with friends and neighbours.

And yet this is also the place where, in 1939, four thousand German speaking Jewish men, many of them straight out of concentration camps, came to live in an old first world war camp on the edge of Sandwich. The camp population was actually larger than the population of Sandwich at that time and yet, surprisingly, there was very little trouble from the local organised Fascists and many of the refugee men made friends with local people. Given that history, at a time when there was as much social and wealth inequality as there is now, there may be reason to hope. But, with more certainty in these very uncertain times, there will always be reason to struggle.

Chapter 12   Religion, Ethnicity or Heritage: On Becoming Second Generation

Gaby Weiner

Introduction

The term 'second generation' has become familiar to me only in recent years, similar to the term 'Holocaust' which was not in my parents' vocabulary – they always spoke of 'Hitler' to denote that period! So, when I come to ponder on what being second generation has meant and continues to mean to me, it is a 'coming after' the first generation, a relational concept.

Yet when growing up as a child in the 1940s and 1950s and then as a young and not-so-young adult in subsequent decades, I placed myself the centre of the construction of a life, with my parents' and indeed my children's stories adjacent to mine. It is only in later life, when I have had the time and the resources to find out more about 'what happened', that the term 'second generation' has begun to have some meaning. I have found it a difficult concept because it implies somehow that I have been adversely affected by what happened to the first generation – yet I don't feel that. I cannot know what a life such as mine would have been like, if the Holocaust hadn't happened. I owe my existence to the hardship, oppression and violence of that period. If my parents had not been forced to escape, if they had not met in London during the war, I would not have been born.

I knew very little about how my parents came to be in London during the war, so from 2005 onwards I spent a decade or so finding out. I discovered that my mother's family came from the small shtetl town of Brody in Galicia, part of the Austro-Hungarian Empire, in today's Ukraine, and my father's, from the industrial town of Lodz in Poland. Their pathway to London was long and complicated, with stop-offs, so to speak, in Vienna and Brussels respectively. How to tell the story became my main concern, which included inevitably, escape from genocide and murder, but also existence of an extended Belgian family, a variety of unorthodox family relationships, and evidence of a range of viewpoints on the importance of writing a family history. In the event, I constructed the family story in my book *Tales of Loving and Leaving* (Weiner, 2016), around three lives: my maternal grandmother, Amalia Moszkowicz Dinger who was murdered at Treblinka; my mother, Steffi Dinger who was born in Vienna and who, along with two sisters, was able to come to Britain with the help of the London branch of the family; and my father, Uszer Frocht, a multilingual one-time coal miner, amateur actor, and life-long Jewish activist and communist who arrived in London just before the outbreak of war. I tried to show the entirety of their lives and the conditions which they faced growing up in Brody, Vienna and Lodz respectively, as well as the devastating impact on them of fascism and antisemitism. But there were good times too and while they suffered exile, separation and trauma, their response was to get on with life, go on to make different futures, and seek to be ordinary again.

My main emotional reaction to my family history is a deep respect and pride in how, individually and together, members of my family confronted the challenges they faced. As I saw it, 'they did their best in circumstances not of their own choosing and lived commendable and principled, even if not always virtuous, lives (Weiner, 2016, p 160)'. In unpacking the challenges and horrors that they faced, however, I also discovered a maze of secrets and lies which were perhaps inevitable, given the tightropes they had to navigate in order to fit into their new countries' demands and regimes.

Family ideology and beliefs

Family meetings were loud and argumentative. I was brought up in a deeply political household. The family were not only Labour supporting – indeed an uncle and aunt became local Labour councillors – but left-Labour supporting, Bevanites rather than Gaiskillites. The debates in the early 1950s that I remember listening to as a child, focused on the importance of Clause 4 on nationalisation, with my family defending its retention as explicit Labour Party policy [Clause IV stated: To secure for the workers by hand or by brain the full fruits of their industry and the most equitable distribution thereof that may be possible upon the basis of the common ownership of the means of production, distribution, and exchange, and the best obtainable system of popular administration and control of each industry or service.]

My mother, who had supported the Social Democrats in pre-war Vienna, as did most Jews at the time since it was the only avowedly anti-antisemitic Party, was not able to vote in Britain because she was designated an 'alien'. She was twice turned down for British citizenship, mainly due to her association with my communist father. I was always conscious of being Jewish, and indeed attended Hebrew classes (cheder) for a number of years. But what I remember most was my dislike that my family was so evidently 'foreign' – with foreign names, foreign accents and embarrassingly foreign behaviour. As far as I can remember, there were no other Jewish children at Gillespie Primary which I attended, just down the road from the original Arsenal football ground. This offered a contrast to Ambler Primary a mile away down Blackstock Road and nearer to Finsbury Park, to which my cousin went, which had a much higher immigrant (and Jewish) intake – and incidentally much better 11 plus results.

It is true to say that I have remained loyal to my family's political tradition – socialist, pro-migrant, antiracist, with the added dimension of feminism, which held me in grip from the late 1970s onwards. Feminism – broadly interpreted as the struggle against existing unjust gender relations – offered me a way of extending my family politics for a new generation with socialist (or material) feminism as my chosen standpoint. Throughout my academic studies and later as a teacher and researcher, I focused on the educational experiences of girls and women. For example, in my undergraduate studies I chose as my dissertation topic, Vida Goldstein, one of the earliest Australian feminists, papers about whom were lodged in the Williams Library, precursor to the Fawcett Library. For my MA, I researched the application of the 1975 Sex Discrimination Act to the educational experiences of girls and women (e.g. Weiner, 1978), and for my doctoral studies, I focused on the educational writings of the nineteenth-century feminist Harriet Martineau (e.g. Weiner, 2000). Fortunately for me also, my interest in the educational experiences of girls and women coincided with second-wave feminism and the research opportunities arising from that (e.g. Weiner, 1994). Sadly, only an uncle and my father of the first generation lived to see the transformation!

Refugee experience

I was brought up in a part of North London which to me was predominantly peopled by three largely working-class groupings: Jewish immigrants, Jewish English and English others. My immediate family – my mother, father, aunts and their friends were of the first kind; the English members of the family were of the second, and the rest – school friends, neighbours, landlords, shopkeepers, were of the third. As a child, my main challenge was how to navigate between these groups. So, one positive legacy of being the child of refugees was a keener social sensitivity and flexibility, in particular, an awareness of the possibility of alternative realities and identities.

Class also emerged as a clear difference between my family story compared to others escaping during the Nazi period. My maternal grandmother and grandfather had moved from a shtetl town to Vienna in 1900 to prosper economically but also to escape the constraints of living in such a deeply religious society. Other members of the family moved to London. My maternal grandparents were young and ambitious and desired a modern life. They were never wealthy and never owned property, and the education of the six children who survived (out of nine) did not extend beyond some kind of post-school vocational training. Several babies died toward the end of the Great War when the family and most of Vienna were starving. My father's family were mainly textile workers, most of whom perished in the Lodz ghetto.

Their situation seems unusual compared to many of descriptions of Jewish family life emerging from the Kindertransport generation, who it seems, had wealthier parents who were able to use their networks to help their children to escape. Some parents joined their children later, most did not. The poor, those living outside the capital cities and those without such networks mainly stayed and died. So a key question for me is why and how did my mother and her three sisters get out, with neither wealth nor powerful connections?

As we have seen in other accounts too, luck played a part. And it is true that a first cousin, Fanny, living in London, was brave enough to 'guarantee' employment for my mother and her two sisters as domestics in her household – although as the wife of a lowly bookbinder, no such jobs existed, and she risked arrest for perjury should she be found out. But how, I have often wondered, did the three young women get permits to leave Vienna for London, with so little money at their disposal? Were they lucky enough to find a Nazi official who would turn a blind eye, or were there other things that they may have had to do?

The remaining family were not so lucky. A fourth sister, Tilde, was left behind in Vienna with her six -year-old son, George, moving in with her mother and aunt after her husband was stranded in Switzerland. In fact, Tilde and George later made an epic escape eastwards across Russia and the American continent, finally reaching Tilde's husband's relatives in Newark just before Pearl Harbour closed all the ports. An older sister died of cancer in 1940 aged 38, and a brother escaped northwards to the Baltic states, unsuccessfully in the end, as the records show that he died in a Soviet prison camp in the East just as the war was ending.

Being a daughter

My mother was 41 when she gave birth to me. She had had a fiancé Ignatz Gold in 1938 before she left Vienna, and no doubt had hoped to marry and have children earlier. But by the time she reached London and moved in with my father, the possibility of motherhood was probably far from her thoughts. My father already had a 'first' family whom he had been forced to leave when he was deported, and survival in wartime was her greatest concern. However, she became pregnant late in 1943, keeping her condition secret as far as she could – as evidenced in the cards and letters of surprised congratulations and occasionally reproach, that she kept among her papers. My mother's sister Trude, some 14 years her junior, likewise gave birth to a son, Alec, two years later. Alec and I were 'only' children and signified a future that our parents never expected to have. So, we were hugely loved and cherished – even cossetted. They could now envision the future through us, rather than be forced to dwell on the horrors of the past.

My gender was rarely an issue. As with many refugees and migrants, education was viewed as a key to making good in the new country – so my gaining a grammar school place was an achievement much celebrated. While I did not fulfil my family's educational aspirations first time round – I married at 18 and had two children by the time I was 21 – I managed to access higher education as a young 'mature' student aged 24 while my mother provided child-care before and after school. In fact, I realised subsequently, that having children early perhaps was the greatest gift I could confer, confirmation to my mother that her 're-settlement project' had succeeded.

Feminism

I benefited from the expansion of education in the post-war period, not only as a student but also as a teacher and then as an academic. Like others, I was much influenced by ideas coming from the United States, for instance, on women's liberation, and tested out my nascent ideas with my friends, in the local consciousness-raising group in Muswell Hill. It was at one such meeting that my friends and I remember talking openly about sex for the first time!! I did not attend any of the WLM conferences of the period as I lived out in the sticks and my time was wholly taken up with finishing my education at the same time as bringing up my family. However, I read what feminist literature existed then (e.g. Betty Friedan, Germaine Greer, Kate Millett) and tried as much as possible to focus on women in my studies – at both undergraduate and postgraduate levels – as we have seen. As already noted, for me, feminism was the logical extension to my family's progressive politics into a new era.

Concluding Thoughts

I can see the reason for the emergence of a *second-generation* voice and literature particular as first-hand viewpoints are no longer emerging. All that could have been said by them has been said. The stories of the second generation necessarily will therefore be more reflective and psychologically oriented than those of our parents' cohort. My parents did not live long enough for me to ask them 'what happened in the war'. So it was left to me to construct their story/ies, as a second-generation investigation and interpretation. I had the interest, skills and time to excavate happenings, that in some cases, the first generation had sought to conceal. So perhaps the second generation has a role in re-investigating the Holocaust record, that might offer a challenge to some of its best-known claims and narratives. Perhaps we are a little more emotionally distanced than our parents' generation.

I have also been concerned about the claimed *exceptionalism* of Jewish experience relating to the Holocaust and its recognition as different in essence from other genocides and human-led atrocities. No doubt it was an enormous and wicked tragedy, both in means and size. It certainly was a defining moment in Jewish history and culture that, one hopes, is not likely to be superseded. However, we can see too that the Jewish people have proved enormously resilient and have made a huge recovery in terms both of numbers and influence. In most countries they are a privileged minority, in Israel they are a privileged majority, and they have begun to resettle in European spaces from which they were exiled. The victims of other genocides and persecutions have not been so resilient nor so influential in seeking that their victimhood be recognised, and therefore perhaps, it might fall to the second generation to demand that these other stories are given more space and attention.

My own *identity* as a second generation-er is complicated. Recently when I attended a progressive synagogue with a neighbour who was part Jewish but had never attended a Jewish service, I was surprised to find much of the service and the people attending unexpectedly familiar, and a fond reminder of my childhood experiences of attending shul! I also found that I could remember much of the Hebrew that I learnt when young and was able to explain to my neighbour the meaning and significance of certain words and sayings. And I have never lost my pride in being Jewish – or at least of Jewish heritage. My family history will never allow me to deny that. At the same time, I have become alienated by what I perceive as the increased conservatism of established Judaism in Britain: avowedly pro-Israel, come what may, hostile to any attempts to find a solution to the Palestinian-Israeli impasse, and all too ready to assert the presence of antisemitism in people holding contrary viewpoints. So if this is what being Jewish means in today's Britain, it is problematic for me – a dilemma facing many Jews in Britain and elsewhere, whether or not members of the second generation!

Chapter 13   My Second-Generation Legacy

Charlotte Williams, (née Prager), Born 1950.

A memory from my childhood: I'm five or six and my grandmother, a very old lady, is coming to visit – a very special day as she lives in Germany. My father has told me to place four chairs at intervals up our very steep and long garden path so that she can take rests on her way from the car to the house. I have a better idea – I'll put one chair out and then move it up ahead of her – that will save me some work. When my father hears of this, he is very cross. She's my mother's mother, not his, but she deserves the highest respect, respect worthy of four chairs, not a measly one chair that moves.

As I've reached my seventies and look back at my life, I've come to be curious about the legacy of my family background, in particular growing up the daughter of one, arguably two, refugees, the huge losses both parents experienced of family members and their homes and continuing questions to myself as to where I belong.

I work as a therapist, both privately and at a shelter for homeless people, which involves frequent encounters with refugees and asylum seekers. Aspects of my own history and identity are reflected over and over again in this work, as I enter into my clients' struggles with how it is to live in two or more cultures, how they can integrate and at the same time keep their own identity and how they can live with intense feelings of longing and grieving for the country and the families they have lost. In the course of my work I am often aware of the terrible circumstances they have left and terrifying journeys made in order to find safety, and I know that they will live with these horrific memories and tragic losses for the rest of their lives, despite whatever they have gained from therapists such as myself, welcoming communities, new friendships and new lives.

In all this, it's hard not to think of my mother, who came here as a refugee from Germany in 1939, and not to feel shocked and angry at the hostile reception refugees both then and now are subjected to and what a lot of hard work they have to do to become accepted. My mother told me that she did not always feel welcome in this country and this perception is borne out by this *Daily Mail* report from 1938: 'The way stateless Jews from Germany are pouring in from every port in this country is becoming an outrage. I intend to enforce the law to the fullest' (Herbert Metcalfe, Old Street magistrate). When I see the struggles my clients go through, I remember this and feel angry that things haven't changed much in the intervening years.

So, working for equality, inclusion, tolerance, acceptance of others different from ourselves, has always been a big part of my life, whether expressed in a political framework or through my work as a psychiatric support worker and psychotherapist. And alongside this, my own anxiety – to be accepted and included and to meet the expectations of others – has been persistent. This too I see as part of my heritage, with its roots in my mother's flight from Nazi Germany and, further back, the plight of the Jews of Europe.

I am seventy now, and for about the last five to ten years my siblings, cousins and I have been rummaging around in photos, old letters and foreign museums and graveyards, looking for more than we knew about our history. Through this process, and through realising that I had not previously told decades-old friends much of my background, I have become aware that I perhaps have deflected attention away from it in order to feel accepted. It wasn't a secret, not at all, but it didn't really figure in my experience of who I was as a young or middle aged woman, as part of my identity – as underlying everything about where I come from and who I am. I wonder how much this has seeped into me from my parents' need to integrate during and after the war. My experience of writing this has made me aware of a certain dissociation that threads through my own life and that of my wider family. My first attempt was somewhat detached – a very nice account of my family and the events but with very little of *me* in it. So now I am attempting to correct this.

I feel I grew up in the shadow of the Holocaust. There were often refugees in our house, German and Russian were spoken around me, news of lost relatives was still coming to light and my father (unusually I gather) told me far too much about what had gone on, which gave me nightmares as a child along the lines that the Nazis were coming to get us. It seems to me that at that time the Holocaust was shrouded in a mixture of shame and shock/trauma, and survivors did not generally talk about their experiences, as we know.

My mother was brought up in what became East Germany – a small town on the river Oder, near the Polish border. She was the eighth child of a couple who were born Jews but had chosen Christianity – from strong belief rather than to avoid persecution as Jews. My grandfather was active in the Lutheran church and my mother and her siblings were brought up as strict Lutherans. My mother spoke a lot about her home town, where her father had been a prominent figure as headmaster of the school, and about growing up as the youngest of eight children, nearly all girls, but although I knew as a teenager that she had had to wear the star and had had to insert the name 'Sarah' in her name, I do not remember her speaking about what must have been a terrible shock to them all – to discover in the 1930s that they were defined as Jews and to have been excluded from more and more aspects of life as the 1930s wore on. The thing that does stick in my mind, that she told me when I was about 14, was that she had been to a Nazi rally as a teenager and she confessed to me, very bravely I then thought, and still think, that it was extremely compelling and that she had had difficulty not getting caught up in the fervency and excitement of the crowd. Her telling me this was such a great lesson in being cautious about judging others and about accepting a person's human weaknesses whilst at the same time not tolerating prejudice and discrimination.

My mother was a naïve 20 when she came to England in 1939. Letters we have had translated in the last few years reveal little political awareness, but it's possible she was told it would be unwise to write about this. Luckily, her parents had seen the urgent need for her to leave Germany and had arranged for her to be taken in by Barnardos, where she lived and worked looking after children throughout the war. One of her sisters was with her there and two other sisters were also in England. As I understand it, you couldn't just arrive here, you had to have someone act as guarantor and prove you had somewhere to go. So thank goodness for Barnardos, who took on this role – with elements of *in loco parentis,* as is evident from correspondence – for many young women like my mother. However, it's also true that they did not look after the refugee women well once they got here, offering them no money and no healthcare. The letters we have seen recently, thankfully kept for all these years by her sister Dorli, show that my mother had to ask a number of times before she had her healthcare needs met.

I don't know if she was technically an enemy alien, but when the children in her care were evacuated to the south coast, she was not allowed to go with them because of being 'German', but was sent to a home in another part of the country instead. I've always had trouble with the word 'German' to describe my mother or us as her children. Was she really German? Am I half German? I've had to say to people 'no, we're Jewish'. They nod and pause, as if they too are trying to make sense of it. There isn't really a nationality name for us, perhaps. And since I don't regard Israel/Palestine as a legitimate home for Jews either, my questions as to my nationality continue. British — yes. But English? No, not really. (As I write this I'm reminded of the wonderful first line of Hanif Kureishi's *The Buddha of Suburbia*: 'My name is Karim Amir, and I am an Englishman born and bred, almost'.)

My mother's departure from Germany was marked by an incident that was to traumatise her and revisit her in her old age. At the border, her luggage was searched and a photo of a German soldier was found. I discovered in the last few years, from letters written by my grandfather to his daughters, that she had been strongly advised not to pack the photo but had insisted. The border police detained her and her sister for ten hours, wanting to know if my mother had had sex with this young man. She denied it and eventually they got in a doctor to examine her. He confirmed that she was a virgin and they were released to continue their journey. I must have been about fourteen when my mother told me this story and it conjured up an image of her being violated that has never left me. She was only a few years older than I was then and this violence to her made me feel very protective of her and aware that she had experienced something quite alien and unlike anything I was likely to experience in my life. As a teenager, she told me 'be careful, my virginity saved my life' — not a great message to enter the swinging sixties with I can tell you! Aside from that, she was unusually broadminded and frank about sex, much more so than my friends' mothers; but I think some fear attached to this event has migrated into me, and recent fascinating developments in neuroscience show quite clearly that traumatic memory is carried through the genes into future generations.

My mother suffered from depression and was periodically hospitalised and medicated for it. I imagine the causes were many, and none of us can say for sure, but I don't doubt that this experience, and perhaps especially the fact that she would have been too terrified and ashamed to talk about it much, was part of it. Once when I was with her shortly before she died in 1988, she had some sort of flashback related to it and I can remember the terror and fear that travelled through her in those moments before she was able to accept that she was in her safe Clapham Common home. My mother's struggles with her mental health made her absent from me, sometimes physically and often emotionally. I had many mixed responses to her sufferings, from compassion to anger, curiosity and fear, and living with this is certainly one of the main reasons I went into firstly psychiatric care work and then therapy training myself.

Of her other siblings, two went to Sweden and two stayed in Germany throughout the war. One survived – she was married to a soldier who had been demoted because he had a Jewish wife – and the other was deported to the Warsaw Ghetto and then, we think, to her death in Treblinka. We did not know how she had died until a few years ago, only knowing she had been sent to the Warsaw Ghetto from her home town. This sister, ironically, was a Deaconess in the Lutheran church. She had stayed at home to look after her parents, refusing to leave when advised to. My grandfather was apparently heartbroken when she was arrested and he became ill and died soon after.

My brother and I recently attended a *Stolpersteine* laying for her in that town and as we and a small crowd stood in freezing temperatures while an account of her life was read out, I realised that this was the nearest to a funeral she had had. [*Stolpersteine* is a brass cobble laid in the pavement outside the dead person's last known address. On it is engraved their name and the word that means 'murdered' and the date they were deported from their home.] It meant so much to us that such care was taken to hold this ceremony and mark her life, and I respect the German people for this and many other acknowledgements of what they did (although it also has to be said that the Stolpersteine project is the work of artist Gunter Demnik and not of the German government).

My grandmother was taken to Theresienstadt in 1943 and she survived. She was 67 when the camp was liberated and when she came to England to live with my parents not long after, she weighed 6 stone. About half of my mother's siblings remained deeply committed Christians all their lives and to this day I have cousins brought up as Jews and others as Christians. It makes for interesting discussions when we are together. I feel our Jewishness is quite foreign to them, and yet our parents were close siblings. That grandmother was the only grandparent still alive when I was born in 1950 and she died when I was eight. She too remained a committed Christian – my oldest brother remembers her walking to church on Sundays near our house in East Dulwich. Both she and one of my aunts were quite disapproving of my mother marrying a Jew – this is clear from letters written in the later 1940s, and although their disapproval seems to be on religious rather than racial grounds, there was clearly denial going on in this family which is hard to fathom from our perspective today. That denial, or dissociation, is so puzzling to me and yet I also recognise it as a part of me. What did they think the Nazis were all about? What did my grandmother tell herself about why she had spent eighteen months in Theresienstadt? Perhaps the dissociation is what enabled her to stay alive.

So, she was my only grandparent growing up and she lived in another country and died when I was eight. Growing up without grandparents, and without a history in England – indeed, with a history of quite extraordinary and unbelievable things having happened to my relatives in another part of the world – is something that made me feel quite different from other children I met. Now when I talk to my friends about this, I can put words to the sharp contrast in my home life, but we didn't talk about it much then, and even when I got involved with the Zionist youth movement *Habonim* as a teenager, most of the other children there grew up without that history either, their families having been in England longer.

My mother did some kind of 'conversion' to Judaism because my father wanted her to. He did not want us to know that our mother was brought up a Christian – this might have been through shame or because he feared we might become Christian, I don't know. My mother was not really interested in Judaism, but she went through the motions for my father, taking part in the various rituals and traditions as much as she was able. By all accounts she had never been particularly interested in Christianity either. This is clear from the memoir of my aunt Dorli, who reprimanded her for not being devout, and from letters that my mother wrote to her sisters after she met my father in the 1940s.

As an adult, I am much more aware of the confusions and mixed messages of my family's Jewish/Christian heritage than I was then. As a child I thought I was Jewish and that was that. I think my overbearing father swept any ambiguity well out of the way into oblivion.

So, after the war my grandmother came to England to live with us and stayed for about three years. My brother Simon was very close to her and spoke English and German interchangeably as a young child, but by the time I was born she had returned to Germany, feeling that it was her home, and to her one remaining daughter there, whom she felt needed her. After that she only returned for visits. They were long visits and I remember her well, although she spoke no English and I spoke no German. She made me all sorts of things and was so capable. She would have been in her late seventies by then and when I think now what she had been through I see what a tremendously strong woman she must have been. In

Theresienstadt, we know that she told people's fortunes by dealing cards. Through learning a bit about the folklore of the camp, we know that she gave other inmates hope through doing this. I like to think that something of her has rubbed off on me – that as a therapist I help people find meaning in their life – after all, finding meaning keeps people alive, as Viktor Frankl (1992) has written. I feel so proud of her.

My father grew up as a secular Jew. I think he had a bar mitzvah but that was about it. He used to say quite proudly that his mother had fed him ham, and I understood this to mean they were integrated Jews, not religious Jews, Jews that look just like anyone else. His family was from Libau, a small town in Latvia, later living in Riga. He and his parents moved to Switzerland when he was three and then to London when he was eight, where he went to boarding school. In 1920, my grandfather committed a crime (a kind of fraud) for which he went to prison on the Isle of Wight for five years. Following this, my grandparents returned to Riga. My father always spoke to us about Libau in very nostalgic tones and it's only in recent years that I've worked out that he could not have known it well until he was an adult, visiting for long summers for many years between the wars. Possibly he went there as a boy too in the summer holidays. His warm tales of Libau were threaded through my childhood and I can only imagine that he, an only child, experienced a wonderful sense of family and community when he was there that he longed for for the rest of his life. I too have sought community in my life, finding it in a variety of ways at different times, for example, in *Habonim* as a teenager and in a therapeutic community and extended friendship networks as an adult. In the early 1940s my grandfather died and my grandmother had to move to the Riga ghetto. From here, one January morning, she and the other ghetto residents were marched 15km out of town in the snow to Rumbula and were shot into pits.

I don't imagine that my father was ever a mild-mannered man, and by some accounts he was a spoilt only child, but I do believe he was traumatised when he heard after the war how his mother had died. My mother said he changed from that day. He was tyrannical and flew into rages and we were all both rebellious and scared of him. He could also be charming, great company, generous and hospitable, but these were social graces – inside the family he was cruel, petulant, domineering and self-centred – and he could stop talking to someone for months or even years if they crossed him (extended family, friends and colleagues as well as us). I recognise his behaviour now as typical of someone with Post Traumatic Stress Disorder (PTSD) (minus alcohol thank goodness) and it seems likely that this normal response to abnormal experience is what he suffered from, unsupported or treated, for the rest of his life. The frightening and conflictual atmosphere at home that this caused made me very anxious. I was always trying to mend rifts – unsuccessfully – and was a child expert in appeasement. I struggled to learn at school and could easily daydream whole lessons away. I know now that I was too anxious to learn – anxiety makes spaghetti of the work of the brain. It took me years and years to find out that I'm as bright, curious and capable of learning as anyone else.

My father lived a Pan European life in the 1920s and 30s. When Hitler came to power in 1933, he was a lecturer at Mannheim University in Germany. He lost his job and came to London, where he worked for Reuters (News Agency). He was a talented linguist and told us how he was tasked with translating Hitler's speeches, which initially he did not submit as he simply couldn't believe they were real.

His relatives had been flung far and wide during the war, several of them having been deported to Siberia (before the war, by the Russians), and he was always sending parcels of warm clothes and other things they needed. His passionate need to bring together his dispersed family after the war and to make sure everyone had what they needed is something that lives on in both my siblings and me. Lots of his family and a few of my mother's sisters were in London too, and others passed through on visits, and I can still hear their strong accents and ways of speaking that told me of another life in the past that I was not part of. One cousin of my father's, our dear aunt Lucia, who spent most of the war in hiding, lived with us for many years and later not far away. She became a hoarder, a direct consequence of the deprivation she experienced in a displaced person's camp in which she was forced to stay for far too long – she simply could not bear to throw away so much as a cigarette end, which she stored in large Nescafe jars, and 40 years after her death I am still using up her collection of pens, pencils, cotton reels and writing pads. We were all disturbed by the chaos she lived in and I was sent periodically to help her clear up. This was entirely useless as it was torture for her and I was powerless in the face of her refusal; in any case, she was far more interested in hearing about my life than in clearing up – possibly she was my first therapist: a wonderful, attentive and inquisitive listener! What with my father's rages and a house full of 'foreigners', I was aware that life at home and life outside of home – at school or in other people's peaceful English houses (as I saw it) – were very, very different.

My two older brothers (Jacob and Simon) and I were raised in Dulwich, south London, with very few Jews near to us. We belonged to a synagogue (Streatham Orthodox) several miles away. We went there for high holidays and cheder and my parents made a few friends there, but it wasn't their natural territory – culturally they were more middle European (again, the Jews in the shul were more 'English' than us). We celebrated Chanukah and Pesach at home, didn't eat pork or shellfish, lit candles on a Friday night, went to shul on Rosh Hashana and Yom Kippur and, long after we all left home, continued to come together for Friday night dinner – I felt a compulsion to go home for Friday night, almost as though I would lose my family if I didn't. My parents were both sociable and made friends eclectically, as did we all. We had a very open house, something I'm grateful for. However, my father became passionately Jewish, not in a religious but in a nationalist way – the idea of Israel and a land for the Jewish people became very important to him. He encouraged our involvement in Habonim and we were keen Zionist activists until one by one we started to fall out of love with Israel in the late 1960s as we became more politically aware. This we kept secret as my father would fly into a rage if he heard anything against Israel, and one Saturday when he learnt that my oldest brother Simon was on an anti-Israel demo, he tore up to Bayswater in his car, found him holding a placard and told him not to come home again.

My father hated Germany with a vengeance. We were not allowed to buy anything that said 'made in Germany' or even 'foreign' on it and if we did he would break it and throw it away. He would not speak to anyone who had been in Germany during the war unless he knew what they had been doing and approved of it, and although he and my mother spoke German to each other and to relatives, he did not want us to learn German. My mother hid her beloved Schubert lieder records and played them when he was out of the house. We were not allowed to speak to Germans or go to Germany and even when I later went as an adult it felt like eating forbidden fruit and I found myself feeling suspicious and eyeing people up carefully. Since Brexit I have dabbled with applying for a German passport, but don't really want to have German 'identity' even now – not so much feeling hatred, rather a sense of alienation from that country and its people.

As I've said, religious Judaism did not figure highly, but values of anti-racism, inclusion, sticking up for the underdog, voting Labour – these were part and parcel of the family culture.

Signs that the fascistic right are gathering strength in many parts of the world are frightening, and this goes together with hostility to other minorities as well as Jews. I believe that we as Jews are stronger and more integrated than we were 70 years ago and should now work with newer groups of immigrants and minorities to defend their right to be fully at home in the UK and the rest of the world, wherever they choose or need to settle.

There was little understanding of what I as a girl needed in the family. My education was given high importance – more so than I would have liked because of the constant feeling that I was failing at it and disappointing my father. I think of this preoccupation with education as common to most immigrant communities – a way to establish yourself in the new country perhaps. And common to Jews the world over of course – but then Jews have often in history been immigrants. Home life felt very male oriented. My father was deeply split in his vision of femaleness – you were either a whore or a demure and sexless angel; and for her part, my mother had little self-esteem and did not transmit to me much in the way of enjoyment in being a girl. What my brothers did or didn't do was deemed more important than what I did and they had much more freedom as boys, but there was a heavy pressure on all three of us to do well.

I have come to understand my parents' marriage as something that grew out of their wartime experience. Aged 20, my mother left her family home with nothing and never saw it again. By 1944 when she met my father, I think she would have been desperate for someone to belong with and somewhere to call home. My father by all accounts had had wide experience as a man and had lived all over Europe, as a student and a professional, but I imagine the end of the war put a sobering stop to his wanderings, especially as he began to learn about the fate of his family, and that he too was looking for an emotional place of safety and rest.

Where I belong is something I have often pondered over. England is my home and has been all my life, yet I don't feel English. I have trouble with those forms where they ask your ethnicity and I sometimes stick my neck out and write 'Jewish' in the 'Other' box. I am asked countless times where I come from, so presumably I don't look English. My family has no previous history in this country, so there is nothing about previous generations in the archives my friends delve into to search for their origins. However, we have found our heritage in an overgrown Latvian cemetery where we had to pull away the ivy and brambles and in the museum of our mother's hometown northeast of Berlin; and we have commemorated Kristallnacht in that forgotten town too, which has now not a single Jewish resident, but where the townspeople remembered and faced in an unflinching and very moving way what their people had done; where a cantor from Berlin sang out in Yiddish on a cold November evening, where the names of those deported were read out one by one and where parts of the Nuremberg trials were enacted in the Church.

My brothers and I are very attached to each other and keen to keep links with our cousins and more distant relatives all over the world. Perhaps that history that binds us and our knowledge of the many who were lost makes our own connections more precious. The need to bring family together is strong in all of us and many of our relatives too. I wonder if an anxiety about sudden and irreversible loss is what drives this at an only partially conscious level. We are fiercely protective of any groups who are cast out or othered in any way – refugees and minorities of any sort. Hospitality in our homes and welcoming the stranger in our midst are precious values for each of us.

Chapter 14   Conclusions as Second Generation and Debates about the Zeitgeist

Miriam David

Memorializing our continental European backgrounds:

We have presented very rich, varied and passionate stories from twelve people, all with continental European backgrounds. We also include three poems by Sophie Herxheimer as they illustrate crucial aspects of our growing up, as is evident from all the accounts. We start with considering our communalities as children of émigrés, enemy aliens, exiles or refugees and then move on to how these meanings and significance of being second generation play out today in the current zeitgeist, which is becoming ever more contested, divisive and racist. The nasty zeitgeist has been accelerated during the Covid-19 pandemic and this pandemic remains ongoing, almost a year on. We draw the threads together from the stories of our contributors to show how our personal heritage as second generation, whilst not being completely consonant, has many shared dimensions.

What is most intriguing from all the stories is how everyone has now tried to reclaim and preserve the memory of these continental European backgrounds, through cultural and political activities and especially through writing about it. Mention must be made of how Merilyn and Gaby have worked extremely hard to find out about their hidden pasts after their parents died. This was only in later life, as their professional commitments were less pressing, and they had the time and inclination. As we noted in the introduction, Merilyn has written a novel loosely based on her mother (Moos, 2010). She has also published two carefully researched books about anti-Nazi Germans and her father in particular (Moos, 2014 and 2020). Gaby has also been assiduous in researching her family backgrounds in Austria, Poland and Belgium and has written a powerful book entitled *Tales of Loving and Leaving*

(Weiner, 2016). This centres on her mother, grandmother and father's lives and experiences of antisemitism.

Many of us have also written about aspects of these backgrounds. As noted in the introduction, Ines has just completed a book on her maternal grandfather's internment in Huyton, near Liverpool, in 1940 (Newman, 2020). This experience of internment was not uncommon amongst our parents, usually more common amongst fathers than mothers. Irena, Maggie, Merilyn, Miriam and Alice mention it in their accounts, as does Sybil mentioning how her mother narrowly escaped such a fate. It was seen as akin to forms of incarceration by some. It is viewed in different lights by us, given the circumstances, and it is clear that it was not a very pleasant experience, and cast a shadow over how settling in the UK was experienced by our parents.

Many of the rest of us have written different aspects of our life stories. For example, Miriam elaborated her family origins (David, 2003, pp 11-18). She reflected on her political journey from Zionism to more of a critique of Israeli government policies in the latter stages of the twentieth century, becoming a founder member of Jews for Justice for Palestinians (David, 2003, p. 189-195). The significance of her background as the daughter of a German Jewish refugee and second generation was not elaborated. This was a lacuna she wished to remedy starting with two short pieces followed by this contribution (David, 2009a; 2009b). Others have written personal accounts and also lodged papers about parental experiences in the Wiener Library (notably Sybil Gilbert and Maggie Gravelle). Peter Crome has collected together several accounts of his mother and father's activities, including obituaries (Crome, 1980;1988). Personal papers of his father, Len Crome, have been deposited in the Spanish Civil War Collection at the Marx Memorial Library and there is an audio account in the Imperial

War Museum. Alice has referred us to an autobiography and biography of her distinguished scientist father Sir Hermann Bondi (Bondi, 1990; Halson, 2012).

Finally, a vitally important thread is the experience of trauma of the parents, mothers especially, and how this may have led to what has been named more recently as inter-generational trauma for the second and subsequent generations. What stands out from the accounts are specific traumatic experiences of Merilyn's mother through her extensive political involvements both before and during the war. In addition, she never got over the loss of relatives murdered in concentration or extermination camps. This is an aspect of trauma that is threaded through all the stories, and yet remains relatively implicit in some. This is clearly emphasized in Irena's account of her mother's lucky escapes immediately before the war and losses during and after. This is similar for Gaby's mother and her many losses of family both through leaving Austria and subsequently their dying in concentration camps. Sybil and Charlotte provide dramatic accounts of their mother's experiences leaving their homes, their family losses, treatment at border posts, and on arrival in the UK. This echoes down the ages. We have also included Eric Sanders' story in his letter in an appendix as what particularly resonates here is the traumas he experienced as a first-generation refugee.

Interestingly, five of our group have turned towards a more broadly Jewish cultural stance in adulthood, with Alice converting to reform Judaism, Sybil joining Jewish groups as a student, and Peter becoming more consciously Jewish through his marriages, and one of his sons going to live and work in Israel. Ines also became more consciously Jewish through her marriage, as she writes. Clare began to reclaim this part of her heritage through her research in later life, and writing about four thousand male Jewish refugees, coming to England before the beginning of the Second World War (Ungerson, 2014).

The turn towards specific groups to find more feelings of community and belonging with people with continental backgrounds has also been expressed. For instance, Merilyn, Irena and Miriam all joined the Second-Generation Network – linked to the AJR and the Wiener Library – about 15 years ago. Whilst this brought new friendships, it also did not prove to be sufficiently critical and socialist to satisfy our desires for more political involvement and feelings of belonging to a critical community.

This reclamation of the painful stories of our parents maps onto the recent surge of literature by second and third generation writers about the Holocaust, escaping persecution and antisemitism (mentioned in the introduction). Saraga talks powerfully about 'how difficult being a refugee is' (Saraga, 2019, p.1). It all gives an extremely important reminder of that period of discrimination, dislocation and upheaval and coming to terms with living in foreign land. It also allows us to turn now to see how it gives meaning to our views of the zeitgeist today and the questions of parallels, similarities and differences with other forms of racism and discrimination, particularly against other minority ethnic and/or religious groups (Akala, 2019; Yuval-Davis, 2019).

Being Second Generation and Debating the Zeitgeist

Merilyn and Miriam, as editors, wanted to give voice to some of our generation – people now in their seventies – who are the children of refugees from Nazism and fascism in continental Europe over eighty years ago. They were those whom we called second generation and were born in Britain. We wanted to consider how our personal heritage and political legacy resonated with or critiqued the zeitgeist of institutional racism of the second decade of the twenty-first century. The zeitgeist became even more accentuated from the racist and 'hostile environment' for immigrants and refugees of the previous British Conservative governments from 2010 to 2019 into full-blown institutional racism and casual inhumanity of the neoliberalism of the Conservative government led by Boris Johnson as Prime Minister. This Conservative government had been elected 'to get Brexit done' in December 2019, 'taking back control' for a specifically British or English view of the world, and exclusive of immigrants from across the globe, in allowing for deregulation or freedom from EU controls and further venture capitalism into new areas of exploitation and growing inequalities rather than freedom.

We had asked our contributors whether they felt they were distinct in relation to these issues, as second generation: such as feeling cosmopolitan and more European than specifically English, including thinking about obtaining German citizenship for example. We wanted to give voice to both this personal heritage and to our particular political legacy. This political legacy includes a commitment to equality, human rights, anti-racism and support for generations of asylum seekers, migrants and refugees. How could this political legacy be expressed in this increasingly febrile environment? And how significant to this political legacy is the fact of being second generation and having a personal heritage of flight, persecution and discrimination? The key threads to emerge from our stories of being second generation are about the development of social and political activism, around human rights, feminism, socialism and anti-racism and links with being Jewish and dealing with antisemitism or anti-Jewish prejudice and discrimination (see also Klug, 2011).

Interestingly, the question of obtaining German citizenship, in the aftermath of Brexit, was not of central importance to all of our contributors although it was to Miriam and Merilyn. Sybil and Ines also mention this as very important. Maggie mentions how her parents felt so British they would not have wanted this. Janet mentions how she does not feel comfortable about it, and nor with visiting Germany very much. It raises too much guilt for her. Others also mention those mixed feelings about Germany past and present. Irena has both British and German citizenship, given her particular history. Of course, several others are only more recently entitled to German citizenship with mothers having been born in Germany, viz Clare, Maggie, Peter and Charlotte. This discrimination in access to citizenship or national identity illustrates continuing sexism in international socio-legal policies. Given that access to Austrian citizenship is opening up, Alice mentions claiming this as another national identity, but Gaby does not discuss it. Maggie rejects the idea.

It is our response to the current zeitgeist that largely unites us, although this is not unique to our position, but we do feel strongly because of our continental European heritage. Our ethical principles as socialists lead us to be very critical of the current zeitgeist, sharing with our brothers and sisters an abiding concern with the quotidian inhumanities and inequalities, linking racial, sex-based and social inequalities and post-colonialism (Akala, 2019; Hirsch, 2018). Mention has been made throughout the chapters of our diverse involvements in social justice and human rights campaigns throughout our lives, both professionally and politically.

Examples of our professional and political commitments and activities include Sybil's extensive legal studies on human rights and national security, which she continues (see for example, Sharpe, 2020). Peter mentions both his professional and wider political work as a geriatrician. Merilyn has been a committed and active anti-racist all her adult and professional life. Maggie linked her long term anti-racist teaching and research, including on bi-lingual education to her parents' liberal, humanitarian and secular values (Gravelle, 1996; 2000). Gaby has similarly been involved with anti-racist education across her career, and has linked it with her feminist education work, some of which has been conducted with Miriam (Weiner and Gaine, 2005; Arnot, David and Weiner, 1999). Clare has also long-term been involved with feminist social policy, being committed to work on welfare and social care (Ungerson, 1987).

All of these professional and political activities have arguably stemmed from our heritage. Many of us have mentioned our lifelong commitments to feminist as well as socialist work, with Alice Bondi and Irena Fick crucially involved from women's liberation to older feminist and gender critical studies. Many of these passions continue, as all have written about how this informs our work in retirement. For example, Janet wrote passionately about her commitment to reform Barnet Social Services, given how it has been privatised and deformed in recent years. All of these various involvements could help with the need to develop a stronger critique of racism and how deeply embedded in the culture of twenty-first century Britain it is. Moves towards so-called 'decolonising the curriculum' is now an urgent matter.

Despite our shared backgrounds and political beliefs as socialists, this does not necessarily extend to joining a political party. Most of us mentioned belonging to the Labour party, namely Alice, Charlotte, Clare, Ines, Irena, Gaby, Miriam and Peter. It is a key facet of Gaby's story and it is important in Miriam's. Charlotte is a member of the Labour party and, like Miriam, has become involved in Jewish Voice for Labour (JVL) providing workshops on antisemitism education in the context of discrimination and racism. We have included Eric Sanders, a first-generation refugee and centenarian, because he reacted to Merilyn and Miriam's provocation by seeing it as a debate not only about the wider zeitgeist but also the arguments within the Labour party during Jeremy Corbyn's leadership (2016-2020) about antisemitism and how to deal with this. Peter however disagrees with the approach taken in the Labour party illustrating the fact that, as Jews, we are very argumentative and not in agreement with each other, even given shared backgrounds as second generation. As we mentioned in the introduction, this had become over-heated and divisive and hurtful to many mainly Jewish people, leading to intense arguments and splits within families.

The new reality of the zeitgeist became crystal clear in the spring of 2020 and has continued into 2021. The policies of the Conservative government have continued to confuse and exacerbate the pandemic rather than alleviate its sharp effects. The harsh zeitgeist was further crystalized with the international protest by the Black Lives Matter (BLM) anti-racist movement in response to the murder of a Black man by a white police officer in the USA and the subsequent British protests around racist public policies and how they were literally built into the fabric of British society. The key moment of debate around BLM serves only to shine a spotlight on how generational anger about inhumanity can be sparked. It is emblematic of the enduring impacts of hurt from discrimination and persecution across the generations. Another major thread to emerge from both our study and the BLM movement is the question of intergenerational trauma, which may have been very slow to be revealed, linked to feelings of discrimination, persecution and even a vague sense of 'homelessness'. We can also illustrate how these themes have contemporary resonances.

Intergenerational or transgenerational trauma has been one of the themes that we have tried to explore showing how slow burning it can be and how it can continue to blight lives around issues of anxiety and fear of violence, brutality and persecution. The therapist son of Janet Leifer read her chapter and reflected that:

> I think somehow, experience does echo down the generations. Personally, one of my greatest struggles in life has been to feel at home in the world. I have often dreamt of being homeless. I am glad to say that I feel the most at home I ever have with my lovely wife and baby. Don't know what I'd do without them! I can't help but

wonder, given the literature that now exists about how trauma can be passed down the generations, even, remarkably, in our genes – that theme of homelessness is the archetypal, Jewish one, no?

To what extent can we see parallels between ourselves as the children of refugees, from Nazi persecution, discrimination, and antisemitism and those of the second and subsequent generations of other migrants, asylum seekers and refugees? During the Covid-19 pandemic there have been public discussions about the seriously unequal treatment of migrant and refugee workers especially as key workers. By the early spring of 2020, Covid-19 was clearly becoming an important global consideration, but the British government, committed to a particular notion of individual freedom, was slow to take strong action to control the virus, with a full lockdown only being put in place in late March 2020. This meant then that all were either to 'stay home and save lives' or be key workers largely in the National Health Service (NHS), and allied services, and although including social caring as one of the key workers, they were not treated nearly as well as NHS workers. Other key workers included teachers teaching the children of key workers, and gig workers, such as food shop workers, food processors and deliverers who were also treated relatively unequally as compared with the NHS. Many of these key workers were migrants and/or refugees, often from BAME communities and they too were treated very unequally and suffered disproportionately.

An example of the intergenerational or possibly transgenerational trauma emerged from the international protests in Britain, with a focus on Blacks as enslaved people in the British empire. A professor of history and memory of slavery at the University of Bristol, Olivette Otele, argued, in relation to the BLM and the particular toppling of a statue of a slave trader in Bristol in June 2020, that these 'terrible events have triggered feelings that many within black communities have been suppressing for a long time, in order simply to carry on with their lives. The issue of intergenerational trauma that is often explored when studying the history of slavery has resurfaced in the most violent way (Otele, 2020).'

Furthermore, and equally deeply felt, have been those feelings of being 'homeless' or an outsider, at very least marginal to the mainstream, and being 'othered' and less valued. Many contributors felt that 'homelessness' was significant to how they lived their lives. What has become clear from the accounts and stories that we have presented is how not talking about the past and the pressures to live in the present, and to feel assimilated have become something of a stranglehold on our lives. This has emerged as another key theme, linked to the desire to take action to make amends. This may also be the case for asylum seekers, the children of enslaved people, for the children of the Vietnamese boat people, or the children of refugees from Syria, Somalia and elsewhere in Africa, including those in the camps of Calais, France.

Here it is important to mention that Lord Alfred Dubs, a first generation (Kindertransport) survivor, and Labour Party member of the House of Lords, moved an amendment in Parliament in 2016 to try to get more refugees from Africa and the Middle East and the Calais camps into the UK. This amendment was passed, although watered down to less than 500 children to be let in by 2020. This eventually happened, by the then Conservative government led by Theresa May. This was clearly inadequate to the aim of the amendment which was to deal sympathetically with far more migrants and refugees. Lord Dubs' valiant campaigning has continued around migrants and refugees but with little traction. We are delighted that he has provided the foreword for this book.

Given that we invited all our contributors to revise their own chapters if they so wished, many highlighted how the dramatically changing zeitgeist in the context of Covid-19 impacted upon them. The period of about twelve weeks of the first British lockdown (from late March 2020 to June 2020) allowed for our contributors to write and reflect upon their chapters and their thinking and feelings about the increasingly harsh zeitgeist. As we noted in the introduction, this was not necessarily a peaceful time but a time for increased anxiety and worries, as well as thinking about building back a better future, and the comparisons with previous social transformations, such as creating a welfare state at the end of the Second World War. Most of all, all our contributors did think about how the pandemic shone a spotlight on the harsh reality of contemporary social and economic policies of the particular neo-liberal Conservative government.

The parallels between the experiences of the children of refugees, growing up within the shadow of the Second World War and the creation of the post-war welfare state, and the possibility of a more caring future after the Covid-19 pandemic began to take shape during this period. Similarly, the question of how to enact a 'duty of care' similar to that of the creation of the post-war welfare state, including care, education, employment security, health, and social security for contemporary citizens and migrants were frequently cited by contributors (see also Gelsthorpe, Mody and Sloan 2020). Indeed, what were raised as questions of intergenerational trauma and 'othering' or feeling marginal to the mainstream, and political commitments to social transformation also became paramount considerations.

Our feminist politics are also proudly held and may bring similarities with other feminists who may also see themselves as second generation whilst not sharing exactly our backgrounds. During the first lockdown for Covid-19 pandemic, some of us, as contributors, were also involved in an online feminist debate about the significance and implications of the Second World War for our generation today and how to build a better future than the one on offer immediately before the pandemic. In this, several of us contributed comments about the ways our families were treated before, during and after the Second World War and linked to the celebrations for VE Day (8 May 2020).

First, there was a discussion highlighting the injustices of internment (started over eighty years ago in 1940) as a form of incarceration and unjust imprisonment, as well as police brutality (note here particularly Alice Bondi, Miriam David and Irena Fick). We have already noted some of this from other contributor stories, too. Second, other feminists involved in the online debate emerged as sharing a second-generation refugee background, that we had not previously appreciated. There were also feminists in the online debate who had other complex Jewish family situations and including fighting fascism in the battle of Cable Street in the 1930s, then joining up to fight fascism in 1939.

The overarching argument was: 'So we all have tales of survival against incredible odds. Sisters need to survive, while also supporting others, who need our support and fighting for their rights.' One feminist contributor to the online debate, in particular, wrote passionately that she too was second generation. Writing under the lovely pseudonym, Book Leaf, she wrote about her understanding of the meaning of second generation as 'second-hand' and as:

> The way the war tormented my parents was excruciating (father fought "the sharp edge" extensively with the Allies). I don't want to invade anyone's privacy, but who else's parent or parents suffered what today we call PTSD? I experienced it second-hand as excruciating... even though born much later in the aftermath... In my father's case, there was a particularly bad physical wounding with ongoing severe pain and

debilitation. Then there were the mental/emotional/spiritual woundings: agony. What childhood can be had in such circumstances?...

Others also had similar and shared understandings about the impacts of the Second World War and the need for a radical caring approach after the pandemic similar to that of the aftermath of the Second World War. Roberta Hunter Henderson wrote passionately and cogently:

> ... I am not Jewish... but my father did fight and was wounded in the war which is how I came to be born soon after it ended. But yes, just as after 1945, things must change radically when this crisis is over. I have no confidence that this hypocritical and incompetent government even wants to understand what is needed, while the exposure, post Corbyn, of the ... devious and destructive behaviour of some at the heart of the Labour Party has left me not merely disappointed but sickened after so many joined in good faith. My hopes are with the grass roots and communities where underpaid and undervalued key workers are putting their lives at risk fighting for this country. A wholesale re-evaluation of social, political and environmental priorities will be needed. After all we have a Whole Planet to save as well. So, in the words of Extinction Rebellion: We Have To Change The State We Are In... Can I just add the large numbers of men and women from the Caribbean and African colonies who also fought and died for the British and yet were not honoured with a war memorial until June 2017, in Windrush Square, outside the Black Cultural Archives.

Another feminist friend (Liz Bird) wrote independently and separately for an online Journal on 10 May 2020 that:

> Having great difficulty in writing anything other than my angry thoughts around VE day on Friday, I was born in September a 'peace' baby and remembering my parents

and their families and how they came through the war, or not, my mother's younger brother was shot down in 1944, and comparing what they went through compared to us and Covid 19, and the war cabinet compared to our pathetic government today, I begrudge the celebrations if the government seeks to prosper by the occasion.

Perhaps a key distinction here between the feminist daughters of refugees from fascism and Nazism and those feminists whose parents were born in Britain is simply the intensity of the drive to right the wrongs of the past, to make good and to heal the wounds by taking active part in social justice campaigns. A major theme of the chapters has been the intense involvement in such activism, culminating in developing a clear critique about how to develop policies after the pandemic – 'build back better' has been a key issue.

An added question is about the extent to which anger about and fears of antisemitism play a part in this. Here it is difficult fully to account for the effects as we are so diverse in terms of our knowledge, experiences and involvements in Judaism as a cultural or religious practice. There are added complications about Jewishness being both an ethnic category and a religion. Our identities are, as we have seen, formed around our responses to our parents' hopes and fears and experiences not at one point but over a lifetime. These are perplexing and deeply ingrained views that elicit troubled responses even within Jewish communities and groups. Indeed, the children of refugees from previous generations fleeing pogroms may not share the same anxieties and passions as those fleeing fascism and Nazism. These can lead to impassioned and yet familial arguments about how antisemitism is defined and whether it is elided with criticism of Israel, Zionism and anti-Zionism.

The issues are perplexing and deeply troubling for us all, especially in relation to our feelings and political commitments about antisemitism and wider forms of discrimination and racism. Many of us may be troubled by the twists and turns taken by Israeli governments over its history of almost seventy-five years. Israel as a state was indeed created out of both first- generation refugees and their children or second generation, similar to us (see especially Grossman, 1990). It might not have come into existence in 1948 had it not been for an international United Nations (UN) commitment, bitterly fought, for its establishment in the aftermath of the Second World War. It is not possible or necessary to go into this complex history, and association with the surrounding Arab peoples and states in the area of the Middle East then known as Palestine and the crucial role of British colonialism. Yet it is a key to some of the Jewish imagination and there are now bitter fights about the relations between antisemitism, criticisms of the Israeli government's treatment of the Palestinians and Zionism: the 'new antisemitism' (Yuval-Davis, 2019).

Finally, there is also the bigger question of how to memorialize the Holocaust and whether or not it is a specifically Jewish phenomenon or also includes, for example, Roma and Sinti, and how to deal similarly with questions of racism and slavery. There are many unresolved issues here around the nature of communities and belonging. An instance of how this has been highlighted during the pandemic and in the current zeitgeist is the debate about plans for a Holocaust memorial and education centre to be built in Victoria Tower Gardens very near Parliament in London. This is now heavily contested as it is seen to risk further public contestation, possible violence and discrimination. However, a decade earlier plan for the erection of a museum and education centre for the history of racism and slavery has never gained the same political traction as the Holocaust museum. It has never even been considered by the British Parliament. This is in danger of continuing to split the various racialised groups and communities, as these debates continue. Indeed, the impact of the intensification of the racist zeitgeist can be seen in a new study of identities in 'Brexitland' (Sobolewska and Ford, 2020).

The so-called culture wars have been heating up during the Covid-19 pandemic as already noted. It is frequently argued that, instead of building a sense of national unity, the prime minister Boris Johnson has sought to distract from his incompetence by using asylum seekers and antiracism protesters as bait in the culture wars. This is also the case internationally, with the increasingly rabid racism, fascism and intolerance of the outgoing US President Trump administration. This is also on a broader canvas, with the development of what has become known, during the pandemic, as 'cancel culture'. The question of tolerance and democracy in political views has become one of moral rectitude or denial of evidence. This is somewhat akin to debates in the late twentieth century about Holocaust denial. This ferocious debate is about the intolerance of views that are directly opposed to those of others, whether about sex and/or gender, or racism and Islamaphobia, or approaches to antisemitism versus other forms of racism. It has become, above all, a moral stance that brooks no opposition which is not new but more overt and explicit than hitherto. This kind of moral debate around values and freedom of speech has taken on international angry contestations, with the barbaric assassination of a French schoolteacher, Samuel Paty, in Paris on 16 October 2020 who was responsible for teaching about French values and freedom of expression. The violent insurrection that outgoing President Trump incited, of the US Capitol building on 6 January 2021 is another example of how democratic values and the evidence on which they depend are now so increasingly fragile and in danger of being violently upended. Some of the participants wore tee-shirts claiming that six million was not enough or being from Camp Auschwitz: a scary portent and a reminder of Nazism and fascism. The Covid-19 pandemic also shows no signs of abating ten months on and is likely to endure despite vaccines having been produced. As we have seen this already exacerbates the harsh inequalities of many regimes as exemplified by the current zeitgeist.

Giving voice to the second generation ourselves has been difficult and complex and inevitably it remains unfinished. Encouraging our contributors to put themselves centre stage and to write about their parents only in terms of how they had been affected by them was initially intriguing and difficult, but ultimately rewarding. As the contemporary debates about the toppling of public statues or monuments in response to the imperialist and racist zeitgeist in the twenty-first century make clear, however, histories are made and remade, by power and struggle: they do not remain static (Olusoga, 2017). Even more importantly, we are reconstructing our identities and our histories; and, in that sense, we are history too. We too have survived against the odds and we want to build upon our legacy for a much less unequal future, even thinking about what an appropriate social and political manifesto might contain a 'duty of care' for the whole of society. That is why we have wanted to offer this account, of how we now see the past, the present and how it may construct a better world for future generations than the one painted in the current increasingly nasty zeitgeist distorted and contorted by institutional or systemic racism and every-day inhumanity.

Appendix 1   Questions for our contributors to consider

This is what we originally wrote in January 2020 and repeated in April 2020. We were thinking of pieces of about 3000 words or more if you wish.

As we are now in the later stages of our lives – 60s-80s – we want to look back, as women (and some men) - as socialists, anti-racists and feminists on how we got to be who we now are personally and professionally. *We suspect that our positioning is not typical.*

This leads us to think about who we are and where we are from:

1. Who are parents were: one or two 'refugees' from Nazi Germany or Austria

2. Where we grew up: London or the provinces

3. What is a refugee, exile or émigré/e? Question of forms of 'flight' or leaving continental Europe.

4. Parental experiences as all in the UK during the Second World War (including internment) (dates of arrival in UK)

5. How does this all relate to who we became: being Jewish, being Zionist, being atheist or secular, being socialist and being feminist and being anti-racist

6. Is there a difference between being a girl or boy from the second generation and whether or not you have siblings

7. Parental relationships – marriage, divorce etc

8. Our present-day adult relationships: marriage and divorce etc

9. Our having children and grandchildren: similarities and differences

10. Our professional adult lives – the complex circuits and changes

11. Our political adult lives linked or separate?

12. Reclaiming German citizenship?

We hope that this stimulates further thoughts and discussion and we very much look forward to hearing from you. Given the changing zeitgeist we think this is an important moment to feel doubly critical.

Stay safe

April 2020

Sophie Herxheimer

London

Not zo mainy Dais zinz ve arrivink.
Zis grey iss like Bearlin, zis same grey Day
ve hef. Zis norzern Vezzer, oont ze demp Street.
A biet off Rain voant hurt, vill help ze Treez
on zis Hempstet Heese ve see in Fekt.
Vy shootd I mind zat?

I try viz ze Busses, Herr Kondooktor eskink
me... for vot? I don't eckzectly remempber;
Fess plees? To him, my Penny I hent ofa -
He notdz viz a keint Smile- Fanks Luv!
He sez. Oh! I em his Luff – turns Hentell
on Machine, out kurls a Tikett.

Zis is ven I know zat here to settle iss OK. Zis
City vill be Home, verr eefen on ze Buss is Luff.

Expekt Nussink.

For zum peepl, its Zufferink
zat kiff zem – vot you korl it?
Kix! Zay sink zay urrn ze
Monopolly on Zufferink,
become inzufferapel Borse.

But zen edmittink to zuffer?
Ja or nein? Pretentink Nussink
mettezz duzznt vurk, ken turn
en OK Femmily to molty Bretd –
chust breese in zat Etmosfair.

Ken ze diefrent Mempers
zair Burtdenz refeel?
Or to trensform zem
fynte kleffer Vayze?
It's uzzervise inzufferapel.

Hef you effer notisst how vide
are ze Zmiles off Peepl who zuffer
togezzer oont sink zay don't?
Zeze hunkry Kitz I see
from up my Klaut –

zay are larfink zair Hedts off,
chasink each uzzer count
ze Ret-infested Zlum,
viz zair metted Hair
oont scheiny Lekks.

Ken vun's Expektaschons
effer be low enuff? Eefen tryink
viz ziss relinkvischink
off Eekgo, ve are all still
frenkly inzufferapel.

For Gott's Sake, she iss kleffer Syentisst also!

I tell him, but vill he butdjsch?

Vot is point edukatink Vimmin? He snortz.
I hef seen zis... zis tippink off Velss down ze Vosch-Baysin.
My Sister voz alout to go, oont vot? A Komplete Vayste!
Opfiously she zen merreetd. Brinks up Chiltdrenn
for vitch vot Kvollifikayschon iss neetetd?

Agathe, I see you so enkry, goink retd,
makink Fistz. Vunse aghen ve stuck here
In your Farzer's rotten Senturee.
Money, Power, ze Gutz - I heffent gott.

To sink I choynt in viz zis
schuttink up off Doors in your frekkly Fayse.
How you Vurkt. Efferi Auer, for ziss vun kvite sensibell
Visch: Lernink. Goink zen et Nytes
to ziss Birkbeck Playse to stutty Messermetiks.

Ze Husspent you fount zair
voz not your Farzer's Pot off Tea.
Vurkink Klass Bekgrount, a London 'Kokney'
eefen, zat ve fynte zo hartd
in Unterstendink off his Inklisch.
But a nice Boy! Spektekular et Fiziks,
Oont furzer, a Person to inkurrich
ze Empischions off his Chiltdrenn.

Appendix 3   Letter about being a Jewish refugee and the zeitgeist (written 22 January 2020)

Eric Sanders

Dear Miriam and Merilyn,

I have read your highly interesting article: *An Invitation to Debate the Zeitgeist*. I am of the generation before yours, so I don't qualify for taking part in your debate. But I'll take a chance and send you a brief outline of my Jewish childhood. My personal experiences of antisemitism plus the historical events which took place, turned me, as a teenager, into a refugee to Great Britain and determined most of my living and thinking up to the present day. It made my life interesting and contributed to making this very late stage of my life reach the highest points in my life. Very few parts of my thoughts and my philosophy were not influenced by my experiences of antisemitism. The strongest influence, luckily, were my parents, especially my beautiful mother. They were hardworking but caring, poor, honest, kind and liked by many. My father smoked a lot. He had grown up in Vienna and was a typical Viennese. For him, antisemitism was like bad weather. He saw an early photograph of a very pretty girl, travelled to the Bukovina and married her. They were in London with immigrant members of her family (sisters, a brother...) when World War One broke out. My father spent the war as a prisoner on the Isle of Man, whilst my mother stayed with one of her sisters and helped looking after her little daughter. They returned to Vienna at the end of the war.

I was born Ignaz Schwarz in 1919, my brother Alfred (Fredi), in 1922. We lived in one of the poorer districts of Vienna. My father's sister had married a richer man who often helped out with needed loans which were all repaid promptly. But I have to state that I knew little of money things or other difficulties in our lives. Fredi and I were too well protected and grew up surrounded by love and receiving all the necessary care, going through a large number of illnesses and some operations. I was found to have a heart defect and sent by the Health Service to a children's home in Rimini for a month and returned cured. I was a play boy, only interested in playing games that gave me pleasure, from marbles to cards.

We went to school within the compulsory state system. From the ages of 6 to 10 it was the Volksschule (Junior), from 10 to 14 the Hauptschule (Secondary Modern). I quite enjoyed those years. The teachers, none of them Jews, were caring and down-to-earth. The children I met were all from poor to average income families, there was no antisemitism within Fredi's and my sphere of living. I knew about antisemitism from hearsay, picking up snatches from conversations within the wider family. The way I saw it, it was essentially a difference of religions. We were Jews and went to the Synagogue. They were Christians and went to the Church.

My mother had social ambitions for her children and arranged for both of us to learn to play the violin. Fredi did not respond at all, partly due to suffering from asthma by the time he reached 10 (?). I recall how pathetic it was to see him suffer from an attack. My teachers told Mutti (my mother) that I had no ear for music. They were bad teachers. Eventually she gave it up but sent me to private lessons in playing the piano. A year later I had an absolute ear: if someone played a note I could tell what note it was. I had good marks in the Hauptschule. The standard of knowledge was not terribly high. During my 2nd year in the Hauptschule my parents decided that I might be able to attend university. Mutti went to learn how to work in and run a delicatessen shop. My father already had a document qualifying him for it. I knew none of this. At the end of that school year Fredi and I were surprised by the announcement that we were moving and my parents would be running a delicatessen shop.

We two boys were not used to questioning our parents' decisions and we moved to a wealthy district, called Hietzing, where many people lived in villas with gardens. The area where the shop was situated was called Ober St. Veit, a former village, in the Western outskirts of Vienna. Many streets there were hilly, the lower parts of the Vienna Woods, the sandstone eastern slopes of the Alps. With the shop came a one-story house. It was quite a rise in our living standards especially as my parents' income rose considerably but so did their hard work. There were no more Summer holidays. Fredi and I went to Zionist Summer camps and had season tickets for the local swimming pool, producing a healthy life for us, although Fredi's asthma attacks got worse, albeit not more frequent. I attended my third and fourth year at the local Hauptschule. I continued to do well, to a large degree due to being a good reader and writing good essays. I was an avid reader of everything that came my way, from trash-branded paper backs to Ivanhoe and Shakespeare. I probably learnt a lot more from books than from school. Fredi and I also had private lessons each of us in piano playing and I also in French. I did not realise that this was because the pupils at the local *Ralschule* (a type of grammar school) had already begun to learn French during their first four years.

In 1933 I was, for the first time, shocked into awareness of events not directly connected with my life. A degree of upheaval accompanied by public violence was taking place. I did know by then that the Jews in Austria almost universally voted for the Socialist Party because the main alternative party was representing the Catholics. But it had not in any way started an interest in politics. The only bit of political knowledge I had was that the chancellor of Austria was called Engelbert Dollfuss. What happened was that Dollfuss ended the parliamentary system of government and, with the help of the police and the army became dictator of Austria. Other parties, such as the Socialists and the Nazis were forbidden. During this process I heard shooting not far from where we lived. The police were attacking a Socialist meeting place and I learned that a man who had lived not far from us was arrested for being a Communist and hanged. I also overheard two young men talking about the fun they had by throwing a Jewish student at the university out of the window. I do remember that I was shocked but it did not go deep and still did not seem to concern me. Dollfuss, as dictator, introduced certain economic reforms but antisemitism was not in his programme. Our personal lives did not seem to be affected by this political change. Dollfuss' greatest political problem was Hitler who became leader of Germany in that year and threateningly demanded for Austria to become part of Germany. This started to be of increasing concern to the Austrian Jews, knowing that Jews under Hitler's rule were badly treated. Even I began to take part in that general worry but it was very superficial and did not change my life style.

In July 1934, at the end of my fourth year at school and the end of my compulsory state education, my parents told me that, in September, at the beginning of the next school year, I would start attending another school in the fifth form of the local *Realschule*. I cannot recall how I received that but I do know that I did not protest in any way. Before that, we were all going on a holiday in the country, this time, a bit more ambitiously, to a guesthouse in Carinthia. Whilst there, at the end of July 1934, a Nazi Putsch attempt took place in Vienna. During it the chancellor, Engelbert Dollfuss, was killed. We heard it on the radio. Even I was shocked. 'Surely it was not allowed to kill such important people' were my naïve thoughts.

Joining the local *Realschule* made the most radical change to my life. The teachers were called professors. The pupils were called students and addressed by the professors with the formal 'Sie'. I was a late developer. During their first four years the children there had learnt hugely more than I, in all subjects. Mathematics, for example, had included Geometry and

Algebra, whereas I only had had Arithmetic. During their 4th year they were prepared for a new style of teaching to start in the fifth. 'The professor will lecture and students will make notes for themselves.' There was little dialogue between teacher and pupils.

But the worst of my experience, beginning on day one of my attendance at the school, were the other boys. There was not a day when I was not victimised physically by a handful of them, who were Nazis. The physical attacks were accompanied by antisemitic insults, such as 'pig Jew!' and other swear words joined to the word Jew. Ironically, as my first name was Ignaz, most of the boys called me Nazi. I was the smallest boy in the class and a bit of a coward. The other two Jewish boys in the class were quite tall and were left alone. There was no one I could complain to and I did not tell my parents. I did not know how to study on my own and the lectures were too boring for me to retain sufficient knowledge. I was hard-fisted and, due to the split nib points, my written work had a lot of ink splashes. It sounds like a lot of excuses today but it was a fact that I received bad marks throughout and I failed the end of year exam. It meant I had to repeat the fifth form. I also failed at the end of the seventh form. There were two aspects of this period which made up a little for these negatives. One happened during the winters. My parents bought me ice skates and I enjoyed the sport a lot. At the school I was able to borrow skis free of charge and every day after lunch, school finished at 1pm, it only took me ten minutes to reach a ski-ing piste and I enjoyed that even more. The second was my piano playing. Although I did not do a lot of practising, I did make good progress and, against my teacher's instructions played a lot of light music, the latest hits etc.

Everything changed when I repeated the seventh form in 1937. We had moved to a different shop at a new address but not very far. I had begun to catch up on my late development and had become taller. I hit back at my tormenters in school and they stopped harassing me. I became keen on my piano playing and reached a high standard. I was writing

songs, lyrics and melody. And due to an older friend getting engaged to the daughter of the

director of a major Viennese theatre, a play for which I had written the outline content plus

four songs was going to be performed there, largely, I believe, because of the propaganda

value of my age - I was 17. And I was going to attend a musical college instead of the school

in the next year. Seventh heaven?

At this moment reality in all its cruelty took over. The threat of Hitler invading Austria

was growing. I realised that what was happening did concern my life. On the 12 March 1938,

Hitler and his army arrived in Vienna on the road around the corner from where we lived. I

went there. I stood on the payment and watched his arrival. He stood in the front of an open

car, his right hand raised at an angle of 45 degrees, eyes staring ahead. I recall thinking again

and again, 'We must get out of Austria. We must get away, We must leave Austria.'

We did. My brother was the first, joining an illegal transport to Palestine. My mother

was offered a job as a domestic servant in the home of one her nieces in London. I went next

with a permit allowing me to continue my education in London and evidence of enrolment

at a commercial college. It was not the kind of enrolment qualifying me for the entry permit

but the lady at the British Consulate, a Mrs. Holmes, broke the law in order to help me get

out of Austria. She was an MI6 agent and became known for doing this on many occasions.

I arrived in London in October 1938. My father had a terrible time but eventually made it to

London in 1939.

Despite arriving in Britain as a refugee, my life has been an interesting one. After working

for the German Jewish Aid committee, a wonderful organisation that gave wonderful assistance

to the huge number of mainly German and Austrian refugees, my parents and I moved to a farm near Basingstoke, where my mother grew food in our garden, my father worked on the fields and I was milking the cows. War on Germany was declared in September 1939. My determination to hit back at Hitler and his Nazis made me join the British Army within a few months. My farm work had begun to toughen me up and to change my values. I worked with an almost illiterate cowman. His skill with the cows was of greater importance than what my education had given me. That understanding gradually widened well beyond my cowman. The first three years in the army, serving in a non-combatant unit because of being a foreigner continued the process – clearing debris in London during the "Blitz" (= nightly bombing by German aircraft), digging trenches in Herefordshire in case of a German invasion, working in the forest to provide timber for the war effort, building Nissen huts for the American soldiers expected and building a road over the Brecon Beacons.

During that period, I took a correspondence course for the matriculation and passed at the London University. At this point I was able to transfer to the SOE (Special Operations Executive) where the toughening up process continued. I felt gloriously fit. We were trained to be dropped in Austria ahead of the Allied armies. Whilst in training there, I changed my name from Ignaz Schwarz to Eric Sanders.

After the training I was sent to Italy. Still waiting to go into action, the war suddenly ended as the German resistance collapsed. My next job was that of an interpreter in a German Prisoner of War camp outside Taunton. My job was also to prepare the prisoners for living in a democracy. I had to come to terms with my personal attitude and behaviour for the job. At the end of that year I was recruited by the Legal Division of the British occupation forces in Vienna. I began to assess my values, my views and my behaviour and, successfully, avoided contacts with any Austrians of my generation.

But I became involved with two groups of the younger generation, the Austrian Young Socialists and the student members of the new Anglo Austrian Society. In that year I was able to mature and decide on what you might call my values. They were essentially democracy and socialism, but internationalism was a major part. Upon leaving the Army, I joined the Labour Party in May 1947. Of course, back in civilian life, the spectacle of antisemitism, returned into my life, although I suffered no personal encounters. I certainly experienced no antisemitic behaviour within the Labour Party, ever. On the contrary, I was an active member, chairman of my branch for many years. I was also elected chairman or vice-chairman and education officer of the Party during a dozen years, or so, and was elected as candidate to the EU.

Initially I had some ideological doubts, seeing the EU as an organisation sponsoring capitalism but my internationalism was stronger and I regret that we have left the European Union. (I haven't, see below) My re-connecting with Austria began in 1979, when the Socialist Austrian chancellor (Vranitzky) confessed to the world that the Austrian people had been just as guilty of the Hitler regime as the Germans. A number of Austria's younger generations began to research what 'really had happened'. Several of them made contact with me, interviewed me, invited me to Vienna to talk to schools, children and teachers, to the press, radio and television. This reached a high point when, two years ago, I became an Austrian citizen again without losing my British citizenship. Since then, I have received an Austrian Cross of Honour (Culture and Science). Last year I also met with the President of Austria, my old school planted an oak tree in my memory and an Austrian publisher launched the German translation of a novel (thriller) I have written.

I am still active in my local Labour Party and have still not come across any antisemitism. Rather the contrary. My saddest experience on the issue of antisemitism happened recently during the months leading up to the General Election 2019 when members of the Jewish community accused the Labour Party of being antisemitic. I took part in the discussion, making it clear that there was no truth in the allegation. Amazingly, the paper concerned, which had always claimed to print all letters sent in, refused to publish one of my letters and the editor lied about the reasons. None of the accusations that were published in some of those newspapers, produced any clear evidence for their accusations. As this took place during the weeks running up to the election, my conclusion has to be that this was no coincidence, but a deliberate strategy towards making the Labour Party lose the election, which is what happened. These accusations certainly contributed towards the election result and it saddens me.

As for your intention to conduct a debate on the world's or Europe's current zeitgeist, I think and hope you are going too far in your fears. I am aware of movements to the right in parts of the world (Hungary, Poland, etc.) but seen from a historical viewpoint, is this not the normal progress of action and reaction? I am not advocating that we should sit back as onlookers. The development of computer communication systems offers great new facilities not only for 'Crooks in the world to unite' but also for 'Progressives of the World to join in action.'

You are inviting discussion on how the fact that your parents' generation having come to Britain as refugees from fascism and antisemitism is tying in with your commitment to equality, human rights, anti-racism and support for refugees. These are concepts that many, including myself, share with you. But can you really take it for granted that your generation shares these commitments? We did not bring them with us from Germany and Austria. Surely we acquired them here in Britain? The German-Jewish Aid Committee did a fantastic job not only ensuring that all refugees arriving had a home to live in, had possibilities of earning a living and were not a burden on the British economy. I believe that the population needs to learn that the fair distribution of the national wealth is an essential factor to keep fascism away. People who suffer economically, turn to Fascist leaders who promise everything. The Jews and other races have always been easy objects of blame for whatever is wrong. Hitler was not even an antisemite in the beginning. But it got him a lot of votes and money. You state that the rise of fascism in parts of Europe is often linked with antisemitism, and the growing legitimacy of a form of authoritarian populism here. You add that these fill you with dread and make you often disproportionately fearful. Karl Marx, I believe, was right when he quoted the concept of Economic Determinism.

Personally, I am fearful of developments towards another world war. I do not see those as being connected with European events but see Trump and Iran as major dangers. I saw Serbian nationalism as a threat, but surely Blair dealt with that danger successfully. I feel uneasy about Johnson. He, however, does not seem to be a strong man, nor intelligent enough. Tricky and dishonest, yes. I fear Trump because I believe there is and has always been a strong fascist element in the USA.

Best wishes to both of you for a happy and successful New Year.

Eric Sanders

REFERENCES and FURTHER READING

Akala, 2019, *Natives: Race and Class in the Ruins of Empire* (London: John Murray Press)

Lisa Appignanesi, 1999, *Losing the Dead: a family memoir* (London: Chatto and Windus)

Hannah Arendt, 2006, *Eichmann in Jerusalem: A report on the Banality of Evil* (Harmondsworth: Penguin: republished as Penguin classic)

Hannah Arendt, 1968, *Men in Dark Times* (New York: Harcourt Brace Jovanovich, Inc.)

Madeleine Arnot, Miriam E. David and Gaby Weiner, 1999, *Closing the Gender Gap: Postwar Educational and Social Change* (Cambridge: Polity Press)

M. Page Baldwin, 2001, Subject to Empire: Married Women and the British Nationality and Status of Aliens Act *Journal of British Studies* 40 (October 2001): 522-556 0021-9371/2001/4004-0004$02.00

Zygmund Bauman, 1989, *Modernity and the Holocaust* (Ithaca, New York: Cornell University Press)

Zygmund Bauman, 1990, *Thinking Sociologically: an introduction for everyone* (Cambridge Mass., USA: Basil Blackwell)

Zygmund Bauman, 1995, *Life in Fragments, Essays in Postmodern Morality* (Cambridge Mass., USA: Basil Blackwell)

Hermann Bondi, 1990, *Science, Churchill & Me.* (London: Pergamon Press)

Gail Chester and Miriam E. David, 2017. Antisemitism, Zionism and feminism. Conference paper presented at Zionism and antisemitism: an international conference, 24–26 May. Birkbeck, University of London, London.

Lee Comer, 2019, Family Tree *Voices of the Second Generation* May pp 8-9 www. secondgeneration.org.uk

Kimberely Crenshaw, 1995. Mapping the Margins: Intersectionality, Identity Politics, and Violence Against Women of Colour. In K. Crenshaw, N. Gotanda, G. Peller & K. Thomas Eds. *Critical Race Theory*: *The key writings that formed the movement*. (New York: The New Press)

Leonard Crome, 1980, Walter: a soldier in Spain. *History Workshop Issue* 6 pp 116-128.

Leonard Crome, An oral account of his upbringing and involvement in the Spanish Civil War and the aftermath of the Second World War is available in the Imperial War Museum, London and digitally at https://www.iwm.org.uk/collections/item/object/80010949.

Leonard Crome. 1988, In: *Unbroken. Resistance and Survival in the Concentration Camps.* (Lawrence and Wishart, London)

Peter Crome, account of his professional career at https://www.bgs.org.uk/bgs-presidents-biographical-sketches-peter-crome

Miriam E. David, 1980, (republished 2015), *The State, The Family and Education* (London: Routledge Revivals).

Miriam E. David, 2003, *Personal and Political: feminisms, sociology and family lives* (London: IOE press) (formerly Trentham Books)

Miriam E. David, 2009a, Journey around my father: Retracing my Jewish roots in Germany, *Association of Jewish Refugees (AJR) magazine* vol 9 no 2 February, p.4.

Miriam E. David, 2009b, My German Jewish genealogy for *Second Generation Voices* 41 May p 4-5.

Miriam E. David, 2016, *Reclaiming feminism challenging everyday misogyny* (Bristol: Policy Press)

Miriam E. David, 2020, A Jewish sisterly tribute to Nira. *Feminist Review 126,* October 22, pp 194-198.

Miriam E. David and Merilyn Moos, 2019, 'An Invitation to Debate the Zeitgeist' *Association of Jewish Refugees Journal* vol 19, no 12 December, p.20.

Tori DeAngelis, 2019, The Legacy of Trauma. *American Psychological Association*. February, Vol. 50 No.2 https://www.apa.org/monitor/2019/02/legacy-trauma

Helen Epstein, 1988, *Children of the Holocaust* (Harmondsworth: Penguin) Franz Fanon, 1963, *The Wretched of the Earth* (Harmondsworth: Penguin)

Grace Feuverger, 2001, *Oasis of Dreams: Teaching and Learning Peace in a Jewish-Palestinian Village in Israel.* (New York and London: Routledge)

Viktor E. Frankl, 1992, *Man's Search for Meaning* (Cambridge, Mass, USA: Beacon Press)

Hilary Freeman, 2019, Why I became German, *New Statesman* 25-31 October, p.28.

Loraine Gelsthorpe, Perveez Mody and Brian Sloan, eds., 2020, *Spaces of Care.* (Oxford and NY: Hart Publishing for Cambridge Socio-Legal Group)

Sybil Gilbert, https://wiener.soutron.net/Portal/Default/en-GB/RecordView/Index/70297# (The Gross family documents are number 1183).

Myrna Goldenberg, 1996, Lessons Learned from Gentle Heroism: Women's Holocaust Narratives, *The Annals of the American Academy of Political Science vol 548 The Holocaust: Remembering for the Future* (November) pp 78-93 https://www.jstor.org/stable/1048544

Maggie R. Gravelle, 1996, *Supporting Bilingual Learners in Schools* (Stoke on Trent: Trentham Books)

Maggie R. Gravelle, 2000, ed., *Planning for bilingual learners: an inclusive curriculum* (Stoke-on Trent: Trentham)

Maggie R. Gravelle, 2010, papers about Maggie née Hoselitz's families, viz Kurt Hoselitz's family, and Annemarie Meyer's family, are deposited in the Wiener Library.

Antony Grenville, 2010, *Jewish Refugees from Germany and Austria in Britain: Their Image in AJR information 1933-1970* (London: Vallentine Mitchell)

David Grossman, 1989/1990. *See Under. Love* translated into English by Betsy Rosenberg, (London: Jonathan Cape)

David Grossman 2020, Amos Oz expressed the painful turbulence of Israeli life *The Guardian* January 5, https://www.theguardian.com/commentisfree/2020/jan/05/amos-oz-painful-turbulence-israeli-life-books

Paula Halson, 2012, 'Flying Roast Ducks: Recollections of Sir Hermann Bondi 1983-2005', (Cambridge: Churchill College)

Thomas Harding, 2014, *Hanns and Rudolf: The German Jew and the Hunt for the Kommandant of Auschwitz* (London: Windmill Books)

Thomas Harding, 2015, *The House by the Lake: Berlin. One House. A Hundred Years of History* (London: Penguin: Random House)

Aaron Hass, 1990, *In the Shadow of the Holocaust: The Second Generation* (Cambridge: Cambridge University Press)

Sophie Herxheimer, 2017, *Velkom to Inklandt: Poems in My Grandmother's Inklisch* (London: Short Books)

Eva Hoffman, 2005, *After such knowledge* (London & New York: Vintage)

International Holocaust Remembrance Alliance (IHRA), 2016. Working definition of antisemitism. IHRA, 27 June. Available at: https://www.holocaustremembrance.com/ stories/working-definition-antisemitism [last accessed 20 October 2019].

Jewish Women's History Group,1980s but ND, *You'd prefer me not to mention it... The lives of four Jewish daughters of refugees,* (London: A Woman's Place)

Jewish Women in London Group, 1989, *Generations of Memories: Voices of Jewish Women* (London: The Women's Press Ltd)

Tony Judt, 2005, *POSTWAR A History of Europe since 1945* (Harmondsworth: Penguin)

Tony Judt, 2010, *Ill Fares the Land* (London: Allen Lane)

Tony Judt (with Timothy Snyder), 2013, *Thinking the Twentieth Century* (London: Vintage)

Leo Kahn, 1946, *Obliging Fellow,* (London: Nicholson)

Anne Karpf, 1997, *The War After* (London: Minerva)

Brian Klug, 2011, *Being Jewish and Doing Justice: bringing arguments to life* (London: Vallentine Mitchell)

Hanif Kureishi, 1990, *The Buddha of Suburbia* (London: Faber and Faber)

Claude Lanzmann, 2009, *The Patagonian Hare A Memoir (*London: Atlantic Books)

Siegfried Lenz, 1968, *Deutschstunde,* Hoffmann und Campe Translated into English and published as *The German Lesson* (1986, New York City: New Directions Publishing)

Merilyn Moos, 2010, *The Language of Silence* (London, Cressida Press in association with Writersworld)

Merilyn Moos, 2014, *Beaten but not Defeated: Siegfried Moos: A German Anti-Nazi who settled in Britain* (London: Chronos Books)

Merilyn Moos, 2015, *Breaking the Silence. Voices of the British Children of Refugees from Nazism*, (London: Rowman and Littlefield)

Merilyn Moos and Steve Cushion, 2020, *Anti-Nazi Germans: Enemies of the Nazi State from within the Working Class Movement*, (London, Community Languages)

Sarah Moskovitz, 1983, *Love Despite Hate: Child Survivors of the Holocaust and their Adult Lives* (New York: Schocken Books)

J. Neugass, 2008, *War Is Beautiful: An American Ambulance Driver in the Spanish Civil War.* (New York: The New Press)

Hans Neurath, *Being Jewish in Vienna*, Department of Germanics, University of Washington. https://germanics.washington.edu/being-jewish-vienna

Ines Newman, 2020, *Internment in 1940: Life and Art Behind the Wire* (London: Vallentine Mitchell)

Ann Oakley, 2000, *Experiments in Knowing: gender and method in the social sciences* (Cambridge: Polity Press)

Olivette Otele, 2020, The UK must confront its shameful past – and present *The Guardian* June 10, Journal, p.3.

David Olusoga, 2017, *Black and British: A Forgotten History* (London: Pan Books)

Amos Oz, 2004, *A Tale of Love and Darkness*, (London: Chatto & Windus)

Peter Preston, 2006. Two doctors and one cause: Len Crome and Reginald Saxton in the International Brigades. *International Journal of Iberian Studies* 19/1 5-24.

Eric Sanders, 2010, *Secret Operations, From Music to Morse and Beyond*, (London: Historyweb Limited)

Philippe Sands, 2017, *East West Street: on the origins of genocide and crimes against humanity* (London: Weidenfeld and Nicholson)

Philippe Sands, 2020, *The Ratline: Love, Lies and Justice on the Trail of a Nazi Fugitive* (London: Weidenfeld and Nicholson).

Esther Saraga, 2019, *Berlin to London: An Emotional History of Two Refugees* (London: Vallentine Mitchell)

Marie Louise Seeberg, Irene Levin and Claudia Lenz 2013, eds., *The Holocaust as Active Memory: the past in the present.* (London: Ashgate Press)

Victor Jeleniewski Seidler, 2000, *Shadows of the Shoah: Jewish Identity and Belonging* (London: Berg)

Sybil [Gilbert] Sharpe, 1991, *Electronically Recorded Evidence* (London: Fourmat Publishing)

Sybil [Gilbert] Sharpe,1998, *Judicial Discretion and Criminal Investigation* (London: Sweet and Maxwell)

Sybil [Gilbert] Sharpe, 2017, (originally 2000) *Search and Surveillance; The movement from evidence to information* (London: Routledge)

Sybil [Gilbert] Sharpe, 2020, *National Security, Personal Privacy And The Law* (London: Routledge)

Dorothy E. Smith, 1987, *The Everyday World as Problematic A Feminist Sociology* (Milton Keynes: Open University Press)

Maria Sobolewska and Robert Ford, 2020, *Brexitland: Identity, Diversity and the Reshaping of British Politics* (Cambridge: Cambridge University Press)

Liz Stanley, 1992, *The auto/biographical I. The theory and practice of feminist auto/biography* (Manchester: Manchester University Press)

Kenneth Stern, 2019, I drafted the definition of antisemitism. Rightwing Jews are weaponizing it. *The Guardian* 13 December. https://www.theguardian.com/commentisfree/2019/dec/13/antisemitism-executive-order- trump-chilling-effect

A. Szurek, 1989 *The shattered dream* (Boulder, Colorado: East European Monographs)

Fred Uhlman, 1961, *The Making of an Englishman: not quite a gentleman* see also Nicola Baird ed., 2018, *The Making of an Englishman: Fred Uhlman: A retrospective* Burgh House & Hampstead Museum ISBN 978-1-5272-1708-9.

Clare Ungerson, 1987, *Policy is Personal: sex, gender and informal care* (London: Allen and Unwin)

Clare Ungerson, 2014, *Four Thousand Lives: the rescue of German Jewish men to Britain, 1939,* reprinted in paperback in 2019. (London: History Press)

Gaby Weiner, 1996, 'Biography, Subject and the Construction of Self: The Illuminating Case of Harriet Martineau,' *Vitae Scholasticae* 14, 2, pp. 37-48.

Gaby Weiner, 1978, 'Education and the Sex Discrimination Act', *Educational Research*, 20, 3, pp. 163-173.

Gaby Weiner, 1985, (ed.) *Just a Bunch of Girls: Feminist Approaches to Schooling,* (Milton Keynes, Open University Press)

Gaby Weiner. 1994, *Feminisms and Education*, (Buckingham: Open University Press)

Gaby Weiner, 2000. 'Harriet Martineau and her contemporaries: past studies and methodological questions on historical surveys of women', *History of Education*, 29, 5, pp. 389- 404.

Gaby Weiner, 2016. *Tales of Loving and Leaving*, (Bloomington, Indiana: AuthorHouse)

Tom Wengraf, 2001, *Qualitative Research Interviewing. Biographic Narrative and Semi-Structured Methods*, (London: SAGE)

Nira Yuval-Davis. 2011, *The Politics of Belonging Intersectional Contestations* (London: SAGE)

Nira Yuval-Davis. 2020. 'Introduction to Antisemitism, Anti-Racism and Zionism: Old Debates: Contemporary Contestations': Reflecting back on my article 'Zionism, antisemitism and the struggle against racism: some reflections on a current painful debate among feminists. *Spare Rib,* September 1984. *Feminist Review, 126, pp.173-177.*

Nira Yuval-Davis and Miriam David, 2020, Intersectional analysis of antisemitism, *Blog for Jewish Voice for Labour*, April 24.

Index

Lightning Source UK Ltd.
Milton Keynes UK
UKHW020805170821
388988UK00006B/189

9 781912 676842